The Good Life

Where Morality and Spirituality Converge

Richard M. Gula, S.S.

PAULIST PRESS
New York/Mahwah N.J.

The publisher gratefully acknowledges use of the following material: Excerpt from *Storytelling: Imagination and Faith* by William J. Bausch, published by Twenty-Third Publications, Mystic, Connecticut. Copyright © 1984 by William J. Bausch. Reprinted by permission of the publisher. Excerpt from "Revelation" by Robert Frost, published by Washington Square Press. Reprinted by permission.

Cover design by Cindy Dunne

Library of Congress Cataloging-in-Publication Data

Gula , Richard M.
   The good life : where morality and spirituality converge / Richard M. Gula.
      p.   cm.
   Includes bibliographical references
   ISBN 0–8091–3859–X (alk. paper)
BJ1251.G85   1999
241—dc21   98-44019
                                                                   CIP

Published by Paulist Press
997 Macarthur Boulevard
Mahwah, New Jersey 07430

www.paulistpress.com

Printed and bound in the
United States of America

Contents

Introduction

"Someone in Nebraska loves me." So read the bumper sticker on the car in front of me while I was driving along one of California's freeways this afternoon. I thought, what a great way to begin this short book on the moral life. After all, being loved makes the moral life possible! For the moral life is really about living out of the abundance of being loved in ways that make life richer for everyone. How are we ever going to live in ways that promote the well being and full flourishing of ourselves and others, as well as the whole environment, if we do not first feel the love of another for us?

Now, Nebraska is a long way from California, but that distance quickly shrinks with the thought that someone there holds us close to their heart. To know that someone loves us, that we are special to them, not only brings them close to us but also strengthens, consoles, and empowers us to live out of the gifts that are ours. It is so much easier to take the risk to love another, even a stranger, when we know that someone, somewhere, loves and cherishes us.

1

As the experience of lovers tells us, loving another and being loved by another creates a dynamism that opens us beyond the particularity of the one we love and moves us outward toward the goodness and lovableness of all people—in fact, of all creation. The moral life depends on the experience of being loved and on the dynamic pull that draws us to love all things, and ultimately to love God.

In and through this love from someone in Nebraska comes God's love for us, too. Spiritual masters throughout the ages have told us in a variety of ways that God's love for us does not compete with the relationships we have with other people or creation. We do not have to step over or around them in order to get to God. Rather, God comes to us in and through our relationships with all things.

But to say "God loves you!" may seem trite. We have heard it so many times that it may very well suggest an empty piety. Yet, the good news of the Christian faith is that God's love is real, creative, constant, and undefeatable. God's loving us is the supreme truth, the rock bottom foundation, the first principle on which we build a moral and spiritual life. As with any first principle, we cannot prove it but we can deduce from it. Once we accept it, we can see how much follows from it. We can see that all of life is lived in the presence of God, is a response to God, and has value in relation to God's love.

The good life, then, is a graced life—a life that expresses the divine love within us. But is that what you really think of when you hear the expression "the good life"? What images of life sat up in your mind when you first noticed the title of this book? What did you expect it to be about? While preparing this book, I took an informal survey of spontaneous associations of the good life. Images that most frequently surfaced were all influenced by the commercialism of our popular culture—owning a luxury car or a mountain villa, taking an exotic vacation or a cruise, being treated with first class service, dining in gourmet restaurants, and drinking fine wine.

These images came as no surprise because television and commercial ads are usurping the role of religion and the church in shaping our imaginations and our system of values. The kind of life they promote is often based on anti-Christian values such as greed, consumerism, and elitism. These contradict Christian teaching about solidarity, about standing with the poor, and about being a beatitude people. Christians, however, believe that the images that come to us in our religious stories provide truthful ways of seeing the world and ordering our values and that to use religious stories and images for interpreting what is going on can help us to engage the world as a people formed by Christian faith.

The good life, as I am using it in this book, is fundamentally a vocation—a response to what we hear God speak to us. What we hear and how we respond are influenced by Christian stories and images. The good life is possible because God has made the first move. Our moving toward God begins with God moving outward into creation toward us, preeminently in Jesus but also in and through all the people and events of our lives. From the perspective of vocation, wherein God calls and we respond, the basic question governing the good life is "What is God calling us to be and to do?" The relationship we establish with God in and through our responses to all things becomes the center of the good life. The mystery of grace assures us that divine love is always with us, inviting us and leading us toward the realization of the fullness of life in communion with God. Living the good life, simply put, is graced living expressing the divine love within us.

Christian spirituality and Christian morality converge in the good life. Spirituality is concerned with the wellspring of our actions. If we focus only on the actions that get done, then we neglect what nourishes and sustains those actions. There is more to us, and more to life, than what we do. Our interior life affects our exterior behavior. If we understand that the purpose of life is to live in friendship with God, then there can be no real separation of the moral and spiritual life. Our searching for meaning, hungering for love, yearning to connect, or seeking fulfillment are, themselves, responses to God's self-giving love.

For many people, however, the moral and spiritual life remain in two separate spheres. Some locate the spiritual life in the world of devotions, such as taking time for prayer or fasting. A spiritual life of this sort can easily become a substitute for vital moral living. But spirituality is much more about our fundamental commitment to God in Christ; it is an outlook on life and the very style of life that such a commitment nurtures in us.

When we separate morality and spirituality into separate spheres of life, we begin to reduce the moral life to sins or individual acts of virtue in specific areas of life—business dealings, sexual relations, making life-and-death decisions, and the like. We expect morality to provide a set of rules or principles that we only need to apply in order to determine the right way to act. In fact, so many books about morality still put the spotlight on individual acts, rules, principles, problems, and strategies for resolving them and then leave the nobler life to spirituality. But so much of our everyday moral living does not fall within those realms marked off by clearly defined rules or principles for direct action.

This book is not about isolated actions, devotional or otherwise, nor is it about moral problems. Just as one's spirituality cannot be reduced to one's discipline of prayer, so the moral life cannot be reduced to acts or summed up in the decisions we make and the justifications we give to support the way we solve our problems. Our ability to identify a problem, and even more to solve it, is a measure of who we are and how we live in the meantime. This book is concerned with the kind of persons we ought to become and the kind of life we ought to live from day to day by virtue of our commitment to God in Christ and through the Spirit. In this sense, the moral life has to do with what also pertains to spirituality—a deeper vision of life, basic attitudes toward life, and the style of life that is grounded in our commitment to God. This book is based on the conviction that, when it comes to living the good life, character and virtue matter; that is to say, the moral life and spiritual life converge when we begin to explore the sort of persons we ought to become and the sort of lives we ought to live in order to flourish as authentic human beings.

While emphasizing character and virtue, I am not advocating that the normative morality of duty and principles be dismissed. Virtue, duty, and principles are complementary aspects of the same morality. Virtues express those habits, affections, attitudes, and convictions that lead to genuine human fulfillment, that is, to being one with God and so with one another and with the environment. With virtue, we carry out religious devotions or do our moral duty not because someone is commanding us to do them or is keeping a watchful eye over us to assure that we do them. Rather, with virtue, we act out of an internal, self-directing commitment to the values at stake. Virtue ethics stresses that who we are overflows into what we do. Virtues link us to action by providing a sensitivity to what is right and a motivation to do what human well-being demands. Whether or not an obligation is prescribed by duties or principles, and whether or not anyone is watching, virtue makes us alert and responsive to the moral claims of situations, often with little attention to rationalizing, calculating, or counting the cost. With virtue, we act naturally. We do not ponder, argue, or fuss. We simply move.

What is making a perspective from character and virtue so necessary? For one thing, our world is changing very rapidly. There is no way we could ever have answers today to questions and issues that we will have to face in the future. We don't even know what those questions and issues are going to be. Think back only thirty years or so. Who would ever have thought that we would now be facing what to do with frozen embryos, whether we ought to clone humans, or how to protect privacy or prevent harassment over the Internet? But by directing our attention to virtuous character, we may become the sort of people who will be able to make right decisions on matters that we have never anticipated. To this end, we will have to illuminate the background issues of the moral life, such as our moral vision, attitudes, motivations, affections, intentions, convictions, and habits that give a particular shape to our lives. When we highlight these aspects of our selves, we are illuminating our spirituality as well.

The conviction of this book is that the good life is a life of friendship with God and that we will become friends with God and with one another to the extent that we develop our character and virtues. This book presumes that the good life for a Christian does not derive from some general concept of the good, such as what is pleasurable or useful. Rather, the good life for a Christian takes its shape from our allegiance to Jesus the Christ, whom we believe to be the decisive revelation of God's love for us and the fullest human response to that love. By freely entering into relationship with Jesus through the power of the Holy Spirit, we become disciples today. As such, we share in the life of love offered by God the Father. Every love changes us, but only God's love for us changes us into God's friends. This friendship with God will only be completely realized in heaven, that is, when the reign of divine love comes in its fullness.

Among the deepest questions we face in the meantime are questions about the meaning of life, about the sort of person we ought to become, and about how we ought to conduct our lives. In and through the biblical witness, especially the preaching, teaching, and works of Jesus, we see what life looks like when pointed in the direction of being a friend of God and of one another. This book will draw, then, on four of the great biblical themes of Christian morality and spirituality to light up a vision of life and those practices or habits that constitute the good life, the life lived in friendship with God. These biblical themes are being created in God's image (Chapter One), being a people of the covenant (Chapters Two, Three, and Four), being called to be disciples of Jesus (Chapter Five), and being a community of friends under the reign of God (Chapter Six). The last chapter (Chapter Seven) will summarize the vision of this whole book.

At the end of each chapter, I have included a variety of spiritual exercises. While you can do these exercises alone, they can be greatly enhanced by sharing them with a friend or in a small group. In sharing them, you may help one another appreciate better the connection between the moral life and the spiritual life, and you may also strengthen your friendship with one another.

My hope for you as you read this book is that you will experience what so many of my students say that they experience when introduced to this approach to the moral life. More often than I care to recall, students have told me that they were not looking forward to taking a course in morality, or ethics. Their assumption was that it would be very dry, full of rules and restrictions, and focused on troublesome problems that have no clear resolution.

As the course progresses, however, many are surprised. They discover that morality has to do with some of their deepest concerns and values about life and about becoming whole persons. Through the course of their study, some find their moral imaginations being transformed. They knew that living morally required them to use their heads, but they are surprised to find that their intuitions and emotions are also crucial to right moral living. Consequently, they have to rethink their whole vision of the moral life and examine the influences and relationships that have shaped their lives. Others awaken to a deeper vision of their moral experience and become conscious of their own moral conversion, or lack thereof. They begin to take their ways of relating to others more seriously, for they are now seeing deeper dimensions of moral responsibility. For still others, taking a closer look at the moral life is as much a spiritual journey as it is an intellectual exercise. They find new ways of understanding God, Jesus, and their role in church and society today. For them the moral life and spiritual life converge as they begin to consider life as a whole rather than to focus on individual actions or isolated problems. For still others, this approach to the moral life gives a structure and a language to express what they knew all along but didn't quite know how to talk about it. I hope your experience with this material has some of these same effects.

One of the themes that runs through this book is that no one can live as a Christian alone. We need one another. I could not have written this book alone, either. Good friends have made it possible. Over the years, many people have had a hand in helping me to draw together these biblical themes and images and to see the wisdom they enshrine about the moral and spiritual life. I cannot thank them all. Some, however, stand out for the extra time they gave me to see that this text would be clear and accessible to as wide an audience as possible. If you find this book readable and engaging, it is probably because of the fine tuning these friends gave it.

Among these very special people are my Sulpician colleagues Frs. Philip S. Keane, S.S. and Thomas R. Ulshafer, S.S., who helped me keep my concepts clear. Mrs. Marilyn Neri and Sr. Joan Marie O'Donnell, RSM, helped me stay rooted in experience and became the voice of the audience for which this book is intended. Finally, Fr. Stephen C. Rowan of the Archdiocese of Seattle and Seattle University helped make this book readable.

1.

What You Have Received as Gift, Give as Gift

As the book of Genesis affirms in the beginning, humans are made in the image of God. This fundamental belief about who we are implies that upholding the dignity of persons and the social nature of being human are two criteria against which to measure all aspects of the moral life. As humans, we are both sacred and social. We act rightly when we support and promote the dignity of persons in community. This chapter will explore some of the moral consequences of these beliefs and two virtues—gratitude and humility—that are implied by them.

To Be Sacred: The Dignity of the Person

The story of creation tells us that at the summit of creation stand man and woman, made in God's image (Gn 1:26–27). Through the motif of the image of God (cf. Ps 8:5; Wis 2:23; 1 Cor 11:7; Jas 3:9), the Bible vigorously affirms the sacredness or dignity of every person. Implicitly, the story proclaims that we enjoy this inalienable dignity by virtue of God's love that shapes us prior to any personal achievements or social attributes (Gn 4–11). If we were to identify ourselves with a role (I am a CEO), an achievement (I am a marathon runner), or a social attribute (I am productive), then we would miss the truth that our dignity comes primarily from our relationship to God. To say that each person is sacred is to say that our worth or dignity is a gift of God. Therefore, a first principle of the moral and spiritual life is that our inherent, inalienable, and inviolable dignity does not depend on human achievement, but it is a gift of divine love. As long as God offers divine love (i.e., grace), we will ever remain God's image and enjoy a sacred dignity whether we sin or not, whether we are socially acceptable or not.

While being so graced disposes us to goodness, no one is programmed to know clearly what is best and to do it easily. Sin is a powerful opposing force in us. Sin does not destroy our fundamental dignity that is derived from being made in God's image, but it does wound us in some respects. The presence of sin weakens our reason, diminishes our capacity to work for genuine well-being, and influences our doing what we would not want to do if sin were not present. St. Paul knew well this reality of sin and its effects: "For I do not do the good I want, but the evil I do not want is what I do. Now if I do what I do not want, it is no longer I that do it, but sin that dwells within me" (Rom 7:19–20).

The creation account also tells of a fall from grace that affects the entire human family. The "original" sin of Adam and Eve makes it more of a struggle for us to respond to God's love and to share it freely. The forces of a world riddled with uncontrollable compulsions, aggression, and violence are too strong to make receiving and sharing love a smooth-sailing adventure. The Fall may have weakened our capacity for what is right and good, but it has not destroyed God's image in us. God's love is too strong to leave us lost in sin. We are made in the image of God and are gradually being perfected in that image. With God's help (grace) we will ultimately be able to become all that God has called us to be. The work of grace can overcome the tendencies of sin toward corrupting behavior.

Human dignity is fundamentally a relational reality. It is rooted first in our relationship to God. Christians believe that we are made in the image of God out of love and that God loved us enough to become one of us, even though we are mere specks in the cosmos. Because of God's love for us, Christians affirm that everyone has value, worth, or dignity simply because he or she is human. Human beings are, as the psalm says, "little less than the angels" (Ps 8:6). Everybody is a somebody in God's eyes. Our inherent dignity, as rooted in God's love, is inalienable. It cannot be taken from us by our own or another's misdeeds.

Miss Emma, in Ernest J. Gaines's moving novel *A Lesson Before Dying*, knew this well. As she listened to the lawyer pleading for mercy from the jury in defending her son against a murder he did not commit, she heard him say to the jury, "I would just as soon put a hog in the electric chair as this." That indignity shook Miss Emma to the core of her being. She knew that her son, Jefferson, was a man. Before he died by electrocution, she wanted him to know it too. She wanted him to know that he was a somebody, not a nobody, and certainly not a hog. She pressed Grant, a schoolteacher, to visit her son in prison, tutor him, and "make him know he's not a hog, he's a man. I want him to know that 'fore he go to that chair." Herein lies the fundamental meaning of inherent human dignity—the conviction that everyone is somebody and everyone should know that before they die. The Christian belief that God is the source of our dignity serves to challenge and correct the biases of our culture reflected in the attitude of Jefferson's lawyer and the jury that tend to treat some people with less respect than others because of the color of their skin, their low social status, their lack of education, employment, personal achievement, or social contribution.

The intrinsic, inalienable dignity of the person has some moral implications. While we all enjoy inherent dignity, Christians also believe that we are called to build up one another by attributing dignity, esteem, and value to each other. We do this in the way we speak to one another, regard one another, and relate to one another. In other words, inherent dignity elicits an ethic that respects, defends, and promotes human well-being and does not count some other human value or function as more important than being human. *A Lesson Before Dying* expresses this well through its portrayal of Miss Emma's determination and through Grant's reluctant, yet persistent and ultimately successful, effort to awaken in Jefferson his own dignity as a human being. By awakening dignity in Jefferson, Grant also comes to a firmer grasp of his own as well.

Treating others as persons of worth is to love them, and love is the relational force that enhances our sense of being somebody, of being persons of dignity and worth. In the way we treat others, we can help them claim for themselves what is already theirs, or we can undermine it. For example, when someone treats us as ends to be served and not as a means to be used, we awaken to our fundamental value as a human being and tighten our hold on it. In contrast, treating others in ways that dehumanize them—such as subjecting them to subhuman living conditions, arbitrary imprisonment, deportation, slavery, or prostitution—offends their dignity as persons. Exploiting workers as instruments of profit or subjecting them to degrading work conditions, or trafficking in women and children deprive these people of the honor due to them as images of God. In short, it is morally inconsistent with our Christian convictions about human dignity to make another person something to be used or a means of personal gain.

Human dignity is the fundamental basis of all morality. Without a heartfelt grasp of the inherent dignity of persons, there would be no morality at all. We act morally in the first place because we believe that everybody is a somebody who ought to be respected and treated as such. We could not have a human-rights watch or claim the violation of human rights without recognizing inherent human dignity. The intrinsic, inalienable, nonnegotiable dignity of the person, not rooted in personal achievement or social attributes but in the very love of God creating us in the divine image, is the foundation of the Catholic vision of objective morality and the specific human rights and social ethical arguments adopted by official church teachings. Thus there are rights that protect our dignity as embodied persons (the rights to life, food, clothing, shelter, and basic health care), as workers (the right to a just wage), as social beings (the right to assembly), as members of a family (the right to marry or to remain single, the right to procreate), and so forth. The dignity of people as a gift of God's love also requires that we recognize and respect one another in every situation and in every type of activity as an image of God and not because of one's place in society. The way we deal with each other ought to reflect this special dignity.

However, when we look around, what do we see? We do not always see the dignity of the person being honored. Rwanda, Bosnia, and Cambodia are shocking examples of the unbelievable crime of genocide; Northern Ireland is a field of mindless sectarian killings; repressive political regimes with death-squad terror prevent the expression of basic rights in Latin America; staggering reports of child abuse and prostitution rings in the United States indicate that the most vulnerable among us are not receiving loving attention. Millions of people throughout the world are not being treated as persons of dignity, as ends in themselves.

Human dignity also demands that social structures support the kind of community that will protect and promote the welfare of persons. For example, working together in collegial ways that respect each other's gifts, sharing responsibilities as partners, and honoring different levels of authority in complex structures are some strategies of community that enhance personal dignity. But practices that foster elitism, sexism, ageism, racism, or any kind of discrimination do not. These must be called into question and transformed.

To Be Social: Made to Share

Another consequence of being made in the image of God is that we are social by nature and made to share. The creation stories reveal that God makes the world and us not out of selfish need but out of the gratuitous abundance of love itself. The social dimension of being human is drawn from the central symbol of God in the Christian faith, "God is love" (1 Jn 4:8 and 16), that is, God is the one who is perfectly self-giving and self-receiving—pure and simple.

The biblical symbol "God is love" has been elaborated in the doctrine of the Trinity. This doctrine tells us that the God in whose image we are made is a community of persons radically equal to each other while absolutely mutual in self-giving and receiving. It is not the teaching of the church to claim any domination or subordination among the three persons of the Trinity. The doctrine of the Trinity points to a profound community of equal persons bonded in mutual relations. In light of moral considerations, this doctrine takes on a very vibrant meaning. Far from being a stale and stuffy mathematical puzzle about how to get three in one, the doctrine is an invitation calling us to relate, in love and justice, to one another and to all life on Earth.

The fundamental significance of the doctrine of the Trinity for understanding God is the revelation that God's nature is relational. Its significance for understanding who we are is that to be created according to the divine likeness means that human nature is essentially relational and that a loving relationship with all things is our highest good. Our very capacity for relationships is one way we are "like God." The moral implication of being so created is that we are called to create a community of sisters and brothers characterized by equality, mutuality, and reciprocal giving and receiving for the sake of the well-being of each person, the whole community, and all life on Earth. The doctrine of the Trinity also calls us to challenge any structures or relations that subordinate, marginalize, or exclude. An interpersonal relationship of love and justice is both the norm against which to measure relationships among persons and between human beings and the Earth, and it is the goal toward which we ought to strive in our relationships.

Simply put, then, to be human is to be related to others and to the Earth. No one is an island. To be is to be in relationship. This is the most basic law of our nature. We have a self insofar as we are related with others and most certainly with God. As one of my African colleagues puts it, "I am to the extent that we are," or, as personalist philosophers would say, "The 'we' is prior to the 'I'." Relationships are part of what makes us who we are. Everyone belongs to one another, to the Earth, and to God. We can say that the basic quality of being human is to be relational, or we can say that what makes human life human is living in communion with others, or we can speak in terms of being essentially social. But no matter how we say it, we are and can be human only in and through relationships.

We are getting this message today not only from philosophy and religion but from science as well. The vision of quantum physics is of a world as an interconnected web of relationships. It sees all reality as fundamentally dynamic and relational rather than as static and individual. The whole of our universe thrives not on isolation but on the capacity to relate. Nothing exists independently. For the quantum physicist, everything exists interdependently. Everything is sustained through relationships and thrives on interdependence.

Quantum science is trying to teach us that we will survive to the extent that cooperation and not domination or competition become our primary way of relating to each other. Yet, within families, classrooms, corporations, and the larger geopolitical world, we seem to be absorbed by a compulsion to outwit one another. In this great power game of "who's on top," everyone and everything become objects to be manipulated and controlled rather than subjects to be related to in ways that respect our differences and interdependence.

Who we are as individuals is highly influenced by the quality of our interdependence on others—human and nonhuman alike. We can't avoid influencing and being influenced by others. Morality and spirituality are, at bottom, about the quality of our relationships. How we live with others is the training ground and testing ground for character. As we discover the effects we have on others we know—family, friends, neighbors, co-workers—and on the Earth we inhabit, we begin to develop our ability to be empathic, loyal, just, generous, gracious, frugal, and so forth. Morality begins for everyone with an encounter with the other—other persons, other creatures, and the Earth. Every person who crosses our path is both a gift and a call to relate in a way that will nurture the full flourishing of each and of all. The fundamental moral responsibility entailed in being made social is to develop one's gifts and to share them with others as completely as possible in the imitation of God's mutual self-giving and receiving.

In developing our gifts to serve the community better, we are giving as gift what we have received as gift. A friend of mine once gave me as a gift an ink drawing of a woman holding a small bird in her hand. It comes with an inscription taken from Matthew's account of Jesus' instructions to his apostles before sending them on their first missionary journey. It reads: "The gift you have been given, give as gift" (Mt 10:8). I value this image and inscription as a reminder to cherish the gifts that are mine, to develop them, and then to share them.

Gift and Responsibility

To be made in the image of God is not only a gift but also a responsibility. We are called as images of God to live out of the fullness of the gifts we have received. Receiving and giving are the dynamic movement of morality and spirituality. Whatever is received in the Spirit must be given away. The fundamental dynamic of this receiving and giving love has been captured in the Johannine version of the great commandment: "As I have loved you, so you must love one another" (Jn 13:34). We are first loved through the blessings of God that are our gifts, and then we are to love by living out of these blessings in imitation of the love we have been given.

St. Paul instructed the Corinthian community about the diversity of gifts that the Spirit had given to them. Paul reminded them to respect these diverse gifts and to use them for the common good:

Now there are varieties of gifts, but the same Spirit; and there are varieties of services, but the same Lord; and there are varieties of activities. But it is the same God who activates all of them in everyone. To each is given the manifestation of the Spirit for the common good. To one is given through the Spirit the utterance of wisdom, and to another the utterance of knowledge according to the same Spirit, to another faith by the same Spirit, to another gifts of healing by the one Spirit, to another the working of miracles, to another prophecy, to another the discernment of spirits, to another various kinds of tongues, to another the interpretation of tongues. All these are activated by one and the same Spirit, who allots to each one individually just as the Spirit chooses. (1 Cor 12:4–11)

Pause here, if you like, to name some of your gifts that are the ways God's Spirit is at work blessing you so that you can in turn bless another.

- What comes to you naturally?
- What have others recognized in you and have helped you to name as your blessing to the community?
- What do you have a passion for?
- What do you really enjoy doing because it brings you life?

Now that you have named your gifts, you are ready to answer the call to give what you have received in order to bring life to others. Consider this short story about gift and responsibility:

There was once a village chief with three sons. Each of them had a special talent. The oldest has the talent of raising olive trees and would trade the oil for tools and cloth. The second was a shepherd, and when the sheep were ill he had a great talent for making them well again. The third was a dancer, and when there was a streak of bad luck in the family or when everyone was bored during the hard winters and tired of work, this was the son who would cheer them up and dance.

One day the father had to go away on a long journey, and so he called his sons together. "My sons, the villagers are depending on you. Each of you has a special talent for helping people and so, while I am gone, see to it that you use your talents as wisely and well as possible so that, when I return, I will find our village even more happy and prosperous than it is now." He embraced his sons and departed.

For a while things went well. Then the cold winter winds began to blow and the blizzards and snows came. First, the buds on the olive trees shrank and cracked, and it was a long time before the trees could recover. Then the village, because of the especially long winter, ran out of firewood. So the people began to cut down the trees but in the process they were denuding and destroying the village.

Then, too, the snow and ice made it impossible for the traders to come up the river or over the mountain pass. The result was that the villagers said, "Let us kill the sheep and eat them so we do not starve to death."

The second son refused for a time but finally had to give in to the hungry villagers. What good would it be to spare the sheep only to have the villagers perish? In this way the villagers got just enough wood for the fires and food for their table, but the bitter winter had broken their spirits and they began to think that things were really worse than they were and they began to lose all hope. So much so, that family by family they deserted the village in search of a more hospitable environment.

As spring began to loosen the icy grip of winter, the village chief, the father of the three sons, returned to find smoke rising only from his own chimney.

"What have you done? What has happened to the villagers?"

"Oh, father, forgive me. The people were freezing and

begged me to cut down the olive trees and so I did. I gave away my talent. I am no longer fit to be an orchard keeper."

"Don't be angry father. The sheep would have frozen to death anyway and the people were starving and I had to send my flock to the slaughter."

"Don't be ashamed, my sons, you did the best you could and you acted rightly. You used your talents wisely in try-ing to save the people. But tell me, what has become of them? Where are they?"

The two brothers looked with fixed eyes on the third son.

"Welcome home, father. Yes, it has been a hard time. There was so little to eat and so little firewood. I thought that it would be insensitive and improper to dance during such suffering and, besides, I needed to conserve my strength so that I could dance for you when you came home."

"Then dance, my son, for my village is empty and so is my heart. Fill it with joy and courage once again. Yes, please dance!"

But as the third son went to get up, he made a face of pain and fell down. His legs were so stiff and sore from sit-ting that they were no longer fit for dancing. The father was so sad that he could not even be angry. He simply said to the third son, "Ours was a strong village. It could have sur-vived the want of fuel and food but it could never survive without hope. And because you failed to use your talent wisely and well, our people gave up what little hope they had left. So now? Now the village is deserted and you are crippled. Your punishment has already fallen upon you." And with these words he embraced his sons and wept.[1]

People who live the good life not only rejoice in what they have received as gift but also promise to use these gifts well in order to bring life to others. Hoarding our gifts by refusing to develop them or to use them can seem to be mocking God. The moral consequence of being social and made to share is that we are to measure what fits the good life by the way it supports and promotes the full flourishing of persons in community. In practice this means that the way we relate to one another ought to enable us to recognize our gifts and empower us to share them.

The judgment parable that Jesus told of the talents given to the three servants in Matthew 25:14–30 is a powerful indictment of what happens when we withdraw into ourselves, hoard our gifts, and cut off the dynamic of receiving and giving love. In this parable the master distributes his possessions to his three servants before going off on a journey. Each is given according to his ability. The first is given five talents, the second is given two, and the third is given one talent. The first two servants invest what they were given and earn more. The third servant, however, hides his. When the master returns, those who invested their money are praised. But the better-safe-than-sorry servant is called wicked and slothful, and his talent is taken from him, and he is cast outside. The parable warns us not to become complacent with what we have been given but to take care to increase it. The parable encourages the attitude of taking a risk on the abundance of our blessings and overcoming the fearfulness that paralyzes us from taking on the responsibilities that we should assume.

You may not regard yourself as a virtuoso of talent. But that is not to say that you don't have something to offer. In the parable of the talents, not all were given five. You may want to identify with the servant who was given only one. Most of us are ordinary folk, with no extraordinary gifts. But the parable reminds us that in the eyes of God everyone is extraordinary, regardless of how little we may think we have. What we do with what we have been given makes the good life possible or not.

The banished servant chose to live in frightened security rather than to risk his gifts. The parable is a judgment parable told to the disciples who have a mission to continue the ministry of Jesus. The only road of this mission is the road of risking what one has received.

Terry was almost like the "better safe than sorry" servant of the parable. During the summer after he graduated from college, he came back to tell us what had happened to him while in college. With his permission to use his story, I retell it here with judicious use of poetic license:

> When I was a child, my parents used to take me each year to the carnival. Before we got out of the car, they would give me a buck to spend on anything I wanted. One year, when we got back into the car, they asked me if I had had a good time. I sat in silence for a while, then broke into tears, opened my hand, and showed them my buck. You see, I was afraid to spend it, afraid to let go because I thought I might make a mistake and then never get a buck again.
>
> Well, what happened to me last year, poetically speaking, is that people at school helped me to spend my buck. And it was great, letting go, getting confidence that I had something to spend. And you know what? After spending that first buck, I looked in my pocket and found another, and another, and another.

Terry learned that living the good life involves taking a risk on the gifts that have been entrusted to us. In doing so we give glory and honor to God and we bring life to others.

A few years ago I saw a documentary about an Alaskan Eskimo, *Nanook of the North*. He was a man who survived a very harsh environment with very little. As the news team followed him and his way of life in the rugged barrenness of northern Alaska, they could not help but conclude by saying, "If greatness is measured in terms of what a man does what he's got, Nanook is a great man." In using well what he had, Nanook not only survived but even thrived in the wilderness. In thriving, he gave life to those to whom he belonged, and he gave glory to God for using well the gifts with which he had been blessed.

The servants in the parable of Jesus, the sons in the fictional story, Terry, and Nanook show us that while not everyone is gifted with exalted talents, each of us has something precious to give to others. It may be a simple gift of listening with understanding, of communicating with conviction, of expressing support to someone struggling or having empathy for the broken-hearted. It may be the ability to organize the confused or to create a hospitable environment of welcome. Whatever the gift, it is to be shared for the full flourishing of the community.

The moral challenge is whether we choose to use what we have or to let it lie fallow and go unexpressed because of our fear to take a risk on our own goodness and on the needs of the community. Terry did not live out of his giftedness until the community empowered him to do so by being a supportive environment for him. Encouraged by love, he was able to cross his own self-imposed boundaries and break through the fear that had hemmed him in. At school, Terry did not banish his fears once and for all, but he learned to live with them in such a way that they no longer paralyzed him. So it can be with us, too. To live out of the image of God is not only to rejoice in what we have received as gifts but also to learn that we do not have to eliminate our fears before we can act. We can just let them come along for the ride as we take a risk on our own goodness and use our gifts in communion with others. To live the good life, we must be committed to recognizing our gifts, to developing them, and to using them freely in ways that serve the well-being of others and the whole community.

Thus, the significance of the image of God for living the good life is that it underscores both the dignity of persons and the social nature of being human as the criteria for measuring the quality of our actions toward one another. It also tells us that to be the image of God is not only a gift but also a responsibility. This means that the good life is expressed in and through the ways we use our gifts and enhance the giftedness of others. To be the image of God is an imperative calling us to live out of the fullness of the gifts we have received by moving out of ourselves and into the world of our relationships. To withdraw into ourselves, to hoard our gifts, and to cut off the dynamic of receiving and giving love by refusing to gift another is to abort our gifts and to mock God. It is sin, simply put. It denies the sort of self-giving that being the image of God demands, and it blocks the movement toward living fully in communion with God and others.

Being made in the image of God and the responsibility to give what we have received give rise to two foundational virtues of the good life—humility and gratitude.

Humility

Humility is a hard virtue to understand. We often confuse it with its fraudulent form, spiritual masochism. Then humility becomes the refusal to affirm oneself, a constant depreciation of one's own talents and accomplishments, a passion for anonymity, a public doormat, a submissive servility, and an uncritical docility that is unwilling to have an opinion. If this is humility, no wonder no one wants to claim it!

To understand humility properly as a virtue, it helps to remember that humility and human have the same word root (L. *humus*, the earth). God took the dust of the earth, breathed into it, and brought forth the "earth creature" (Gn 2:7). We have been destined for humility ever since: "Remember that you are dust and unto dust you shall return." Humility, simply put, is being down to earth about yourself.

It is the virtue of being honest to God about yourself. Humility is not having a talent and then doing your best to deny it; rather, it is the realistic acceptance of your power and limitations, of what you can do and what you cannot do. A professor of mine gave the best functional definition of humility I have ever heard. "Humility," he said, "is the willingness to be who you are and to do what you can." This clearly situates humility between the extremes of pride (acting as though I had no limits) and self-effacement (ignoring my real ability and accomplishments).

Humility is the willingness to be who we are. Who are we? Being made in the image of God tells us that we are creatures, not the Creator. We are gifted, but we are not all-gifted. We can do some things, but we can't do everything. We are dependent, not self-sufficient. Everything is pure grace. Our very physical being depended on others to come to be. That we continue to survive depends on the care and know-how of others. We eat what others have sown, harvested, and often cooked for us. We speak a language others have coined. We enjoy rights for which others have died. To be so gifted is not to be humiliated, but it is to be invited to participate in sharing these gifts with others who also depend upon us.

No wonder humility does not come easy to us. We bridle at limits and dependence. The ideal self that our culture upholds is one whose dignity depends on an independent ability to control outcomes. Humility forces us to ask, "To what extent is living with independent, absolute control the only kind of life worth living?" How much is the need to control coming from fear and anxiety? Certainly no one wants to deny that we need some degree of freedom and control if we are to respect our personal dignity. In modern medicine, for example, we must be able to have some control in making decisions; otherwise, we could easily be used and abused by the technological domination of medicine.

But the freedom we prize and protect is less the freedom to control outcomes and more the freedom to choose an attitude. Viktor Frankl, in his reflection on surviving the concentration camps, called the capacity to remain our own person in the face of what is given us the "last of the human freedoms—to choose one's attitude in any given set of circumstances, to choose one's own way."[2] This is the freedom born out of the virtue of humility.

Humility's role in our spiritual tradition of asceticism, with its spirit of detachment, can make a needed contribution to discussions about how we face death, how to care for the dying, and whether we need to resort to assisted suicide. Humility checks our passion for control by enabling us to take a lighter grasp on life, to live with limits, to choose to play the hand we have been handed, and to stand back and let go of what cannot be ours. As mortal persons, we must face the fact that life is inevitably marked by illness, aging, decline, and death. The humble know that our bodies will ultimately go their own way and follow their own internal dynamism. To die with dignity, the humble do not need to be in charge of every detail. They only need to be in charge of their interior self so as to integrate into life the unexpected as well as the inevitable.

Moreover, humility does not regard as an indignity the dependence that comes with aging, sickness, and dying. Accepting dependence can be a growing process, not a wilting one. Jesus showed in his suffering the dignity of dependence. In Gethsemane, we hear him plead with his disciples, "The sorrow in my heart is so great that it almost crushes me. Stay here and keep watch with me" (Mt 26:38). This dependence on others is a sign of a more radical dependence on God, for Jesus then threw himself on the ground and prayed, "My Father, if it is possible, take this cup of suffering from me! Yet not what I want, but what you want" (Mt 26:39). Jesus shows that dependence is a call to be open to God, to see more clearly the limits of control. Humility recognizes that leaning on the strength of others and being open to their care is a necessary grace for living and dying well.

So the fact that we are limited and dependent is clear. The question for humility as a virtue is, is that okay with us? Do we resent having to ask for help? Are we open to what we don't know or can't do? Do we lose our dignity and worth if we don't have absolute control? Do we find it hard to accept a gift? To say "Thank you"? For example, you have just finished the best round of golf in your life, shooting seven under par. What's the most humble thing you can say to those who congratulate you? "Oh, it was nothing. I was just lucky today," or, "You shot a good round, too." Neither. Humility simply says, "Thanks." We make no excuses. We own what we did and it's great. The humble are able to consent to, affirm, and celebrate who they are.

Humility is also the willingness to do what we can. We are able to be part of the action, but we are also able to let go of what is beyond our control. Humility does not try to run ahead of our graces and make of ourselves more than we are. Humility graciously accepts ourselves as creatures and God as Creator. With humility, we are able to contribute what we can and then stand back when it is time and trust in the gracious work of God and in the gifts of others. This may seem like a simple formula for the good life, but it often takes serious illness or death to impress the idea on our minds. Serious illness reminds us that we are mortal "vessels of clay" (2 Cor 4:7), fragile, and ultimately powerless. Only God is without limit.

Signs that we are running ahead of our graces are behaviors such as growing cynical, anxious, depressed, highly critical of others, defensive, short-tempered, and suspicious of the basic honesty and goodwill of others. When we start to show signs like these, we need to ask just how much of the situation bothers us for objective reasons and how much bothers us because it reminds us of our own limitations that we don't want to accept. Without humility we tend to exaggerate our importance and put down others so that we feel more valuable. People who can't live with themselves as they are seem to try to do their best to make sure others can't either. Humility would keep us honest with what is troubling us so that we can deal with it as it is and not look for a scapegoat in other issues or other people.

The deadly enemy of humility is pride, the vice of thinking and acting as if one had no limits. Pride is grossly competitive, unable to enjoy an achievement for its own worth but only to the extent that it is better than someone else's achievement. The proud cannot take delight in anything for its own sake but only because it is good by comparison. With a posture like that, the proud make their gifts become walls that alienate rather than bridges that unite. Humility, on the other hand, enables us to affirm and celebrate what we have, to recognize that even if we don't have it all we are still secure enough and good enough, and then to be open to receive what others want to give.

Gratitude

Gratitude follows closely on humility that accepts that we are ever blessed with gifts to share. Gratitude is the virtue that gladly recognizes everything we have received as gifts to be shared, not possessions to be hoarded. Gratitude remembers, too, that God is the giver of these gifts. Remembering, in fact, is what gratitude likes to do best. Remembering is the way of letting the love of God touch us again as we relive those graced moments of our lives. When we sit back and look over all that we have received and see where others have extended themselves to us, we see the work of God's grace in our lives. It is no accident that *think* and *thank* come from the same root word (L. *tongere,* to know). The experience of God's giving graciously—think about that—calls forth gratitude—thanks—as a pivotal virtue of the moral life. Praise and thanks are fundamental Christian attitudes. No wonder we put the Eucharist at the heart of the Christian moral and spiritual life. As the preface to the eucharistic prayer says, we are "always and everywhere to give thanks." In thankfulness to God for gifts freely bestowed, a eucharistic spirituality and morality cares for what has been given to us and shares our gifts for the well-being of all.

Gratitude as a virtue is a disciplined way of living. The choice to be grateful does not come without effort. It is difficult to be grateful to God, for example, when those whom we most love are brutally taken away in an act of random violence or when all that we worked for in building a home is destroyed by an earthquake, flood, or mudslide. We could always point to those who are better off, or we could pity ourselves for having gotten the worst of it. We can look for what is missing in our lives or rehearse the "if onlys" that would have made everything turn out differently. But gratitude looks over life and notices that much of who we are is not our doing. It comes as a gift of God and of caring and supportive friends. This is what Terry, our college graduate, discovered. Each time we choose to be grateful, the next choice is a little easier, a little less self-conscious. When we reach into our pockets, we find another buck to spend, and then another, and another. It's great, and we are grateful.

Grateful people are, at the bottom, happy with themselves, with others, and with what they have. They know that they are blessed beyond their deserving. Even under adverse conditions, grateful people are not miserable. They can wrap themselves in resentment if they want, but they choose not to for they still have a thousand reasons to thank God for the good experiences of the past, even though these may have come in small sizes and with less frequency than they desire. This means that gratitude is a choice we make to respond to whatever happens to us with an openness that receives it as a grace. When we recognize that what we have comes to us more as gift than as achievement, then we need not be defensive and violent, but we can freely give as gift what we have received as gift.

Spiritual Exercises

♦ In a quiet place, repeat the title of this chapter, "What you have received as gift, give as gift," as a mantra or breath prayer. Rest with this for a moment.

♦ Read Ernest J. Gaines's novel, *A Lesson Before Dying.* How does it strike you? What "lesson" does it teach you?

♦ Draw a series of five or six concentric circles. Put yourself in the center. In each circle moving out from you, write the names of those who make up the range of relationships that influence you, starting with those who have the most influence and moving out to those with less. For example, you might include in these circles family, close friends, mentors, social companions, colleagues, those for whom you work, those in the various communities to which you belong.

♦ What do you "receive" from each of these circles? What do you "give" to each?

♦ In what ways are those in each circle a "gift" to you? To what do they "call" you?

◆ The chapter invited you to an exercise of naming your gifts, or blessings from God. Take time now to count your blessings. Make a list of what comes to you naturally, what you have a passion for, what you enjoy doing, what others seem to ask of you frequently. If you do this exercise in a group, you might want to close with a litany of blessing for one another.

◆ Read Terry's story again from this chapter. What "buck" are you clutching in your fist? Who will set you free so that you can spend it?

◆ Humility is being down to earth about yourself. In what areas do you find it hard to let go, to accept your limits, to ask for help? In what areas of your life do you show a need for excessive control and independence?

◆ Remembering is what gratitude likes to do best. Write a thank-you note to someone who has especially touched your life this past year. You don't necessarily have to mail it. Just writing it helps you to remember this graced moment with gratitude.

2.

I Have Called You By Name; You Are Precious to Me

Complementary to understanding the human person as the image of God is the moral vision of the covenant. The claims that we make about who we ought to be as the image of God presuppose a way of relating to God and to one another. The covenant describes that relationship. It is a relationship of God's faithful abiding love for us inviting a like response from us. Because the covenant is a complex reality with many aspects, I am necessarily being selective in these next three chapters when I hold up as especially informative of the good life only three features of covenantal life—worth, solidarity, and fidelity. This chapter will reflect on covenantal love that establishes our worth and its corresponding virtue—self-esteem.

Worth

Our hearts hunger for love. We have a passionate longing to know that we count in the eyes of someone special.

We long to know that we are loved and valued and are the source of delight for another. Our anger, hatred, and fear are inverted desires for a love that we have not been able to receive. "Do you love me?" is the persistent cry of the heart. We ask it not just of people significant to us but ultimately of God. Through the covenant, God responds to this cry of the heart's longing for worth with a firm "yes." "I have called you by name, you are mine....I will give up whole nations to save your life, because you are precious to me and because I love you and give you honor" (Is 43:1, 4).

The covenant recalls that grace is the first move. We are not so much the searchers as the ones searched for. Because God has taken the initiative to enter into covenant with us, we matter to God in a most serious way. Such love bestows worth. Our worth is first given to us; then it is claimed. Our true, ultimate worth comes primarily from God's loving us, and not from our personal achievements or social roles.

In the New Testament, one of the favorite images of Jesus for those whose lives are grounded in God's unconditional love is the child. When Jesus is asked who is the greatest in God's reign, he reaches into the crowd, sets a child beside him, and says, in effect, "Unless you become like this, you will never understand greatness" (cf. Mt 18:1–5). What makes the child such an apt image is that the child's worth and security are grounded in the generous love of the parents and not in something the child has achieved. That is what we are like before God. We are grounded in a love that desires us out of the abundance of love itself and not because of anything we may have accomplished.

Our fundamental, biblically informed insight is that our worth and security are grounded in the unconditional love of God. Yet, whom do we let name us? To whom do we feel we really belong? There are so many voices wanting to claim us. To whom do we listen?

Before Jesus began his public ministry he was tempted in the desert by seductive voices full of promise (Mt 4:1–11). These voices promised him security if he could prove his worth by being successful, popular, and powerful. Such promises are indeed seductive for anyone who would doubt his or her own goodness and worth. Jesus was able to resist the temptations because he heard in the center of his heart the voice of love that named him and defined his mission. He believed in the word of divine love and lived true to its liberating power.

The voices that surround us today try to convince us that we are not good but that we can become good if we succeed at a few things. In a world that constantly compares, it is hard to believe that there is a love that does not do the same. In a culture that raises trophy children and is full of grades, scores, ranks and statistics, it is hard to believe that there is love that does not measure us one against the other. The love that compares is a love filled with *ifs*. You are a person of worth if you are educated, if you have a good job, if you accumulate wealth, power, position, and prestige. These endless *ifs* only enslave us. We can give freely what we have freely received only when we know ourselves to be fully accepted by a love that makes no conditions. But so much of our love is compromised by conditions. No wonder we need a special word to describe the love for which we long. We call it *unconditional* love. Only *love* without conditions communicates the love we long for.

The conditions that compromise love make us doubt that our worth is grounded in a love beyond measure. So we reach for our trophies, name our triumphs, or cite our awards to say, "See, I am worthy of love." Without being grounded in a love beyond measure, we become swamped by so many needs and wants that we become suspicious of every voice. We wonder if anyone truly loves us. What might be generosity seems like manipulation. We don't want to be used. We wonder if we ourselves can love. What looks like an offer of love is really a cry for affection—do you love me? But when we discover that our true nature is to be loveable and loving, then we can embrace the whole world in freedom and without fear. When we accept ourselves as people who are already loved the way God loves us—completely and unconditionally—then we can give to others what they need without manipulating them in order to win love in return.

Self-Esteem

In our fragmented world, we are so keenly aware of the lack of love and the abundance of hatred, cruelty, and indifference that prevails. Not being able to hear the voice of love that grounds our worth only spells tragedy for living the good life. Self-esteem is the virtue by which we accept ourselves as being worthwhile apart from our achievements. It is a principal virtue that makes the good life possible. One of the greatest things we can do for others is to like ourselves, to really enjoy being who we are and doing what we can. That takes a healthy sense of self. That takes hearing the voice of unconditional love, believing it to be true, and then living in ways that show that we like what we have heard and have come to know.

The image we have of ourselves is largely a product of what others have told us that we are. The IRS knows me by my social security number. I have no personality. The company says that I am an employee. There I am valued for what I do. The kids say that I am an old man or an old lady. For them I am out of touch and out of joint. The image we have of ourselves will show up in our conduct, for we tend to shape our behavior out of the way we are named or labeled. Names that affirm (you are the sunshine of my life) call forth the best in us, whereas names that condemn or put down (you are such a jerk) have the opposite effect. So, for the good life, it makes a great deal of difference how others relate to us, how they name us, what image we have of ourselves as a result, and how we value ourselves in that image. Another's esteem for us nurtures self-esteem.

The familiar fairy tale of Rapunzel can be taken as a story about self-image, its sources, and its effects on our conduct. It shows us that how we see ourself in the eyes of another is a crucial part of self-esteem. In this story a young girl with long hair is imprisoned in a tower with an old witch. The girl is really very beautiful, but the witch consistently tells her that she is ugly. That is the witch's strategy to keep the girl inside. Rapunzel is imprisoned not so much by the tower but by the fear of her own ugliness that the witch keeps before her. Rapunzel's liberation comes when she lets down her hair to the young prince below who recognizes her beauty, names it for her, and by this sets her free. Not until Rapunzel sees in the mirror of the prince's eyes that she is beautiful—and accepts what she sees—can she free herself from the imprisonment of her self-image as ugly and unwanted.

Now, contrast the story of Rapunzel with the experience expressed by Ysaye Maria Barnwell in her song, "No Mirrors in My Nana's House." In this song, a black woman sings of seeing the beauty of everything, especially herself, through her Nana's eyes. Without mirrors, she can only see herself the way her Nana tells her that she is. In her Nana's eyes, her black skin, her flat nose, and her frumpy, baggy clothes are all beautiful. Through her Nana's eyes, she lives in a kind of magical world where she only knows love. She doesn't know hate.

Sadly, however, not many people can sing this song as their own. Coming to a sense of self through the eyes of unconditional love has not been everyone's experience. We feel valuable when we know someone loves us. Too many, unfortunately, live unsure that they are loved as they are. "I hate myself" is their prevailing attitude. They live burdened by an abiding sense that they are not worth much to anyone, not even to themselves.

Then there are those who have a sense of self-worth, but they know how fragile this gift is. They can easily feel bad about themselves because they have not done enough to measure up, or they might believe that whatever they have done has been filled only with mistakes. Rather than accept the fact that mistakes are an inevitable part of everyone's life, they can easily make them the measure of their worth and so erode their self-esteem.

Many factors can account for making low self-esteem the rule rather than the exception in people's lives. What becomes a person's self-esteem is developed primarily through relationships, especially our most influential ones. That is why a smile of recognition and a kind word of affirmation are so important. If love can build up, cruelty, unkindness, inattention can bruise deeply, or even destroy. Horror stories abound of parents who did not give to children the affirmation and encouragement they needed, of teachers who mistreated them, or of friends who betrayed them. Their lives are filled more with criticism and rejection than with encouragement and acceptance. They can easily identify with Vivian's feelings in the film *Pretty Woman.* After telling of how her mother mistreated her as a child by locking her in the attic as a punishment, Vivian says, "When people put you down enough, you start to believe it. The bad stuff is easier to believe."

Low self-esteem may also result from being subjected to prejudice and oppression within society when, for example, male dominated structures do not honor women's gifts or when Caucasian-dominated structures oppress people of color. A lack of self-esteem can also contribute to unrealized hopes, undiscovered talents, unborn dreams. In the movie *Shirley Valentine,* we see this played out in the life of the protagonist. In one scene, as she sits by the seaside in Greece, reflecting on her own life and how little and unused it has been, Shirley says, "I've allowed myself to lead a little life while inside me there is so much more…it's gone unused and now it never will be. Why do we get all this life if we never use it? Why do we get all these feelings and dreams and hopes if we don't ever use them?"

Religious preaching and teaching can also impede our quest for self-esteem. Our beliefs about God correlate with our self image. What image of God do you carry around? Where did you get it? Most of us have picked up our images of God from the way we have been taught about God, especially through the way we have been treated in the name of God and according to God's will. Our images of God are hard to shake. They seem to have embedded themselves in the elusive corners of our subconscious and continue to influence our convictions about God and about ourselves. They especially influence our feeling for what it is like to live in relationship to God, and they affect our attitudes toward the moral life as well.

So we need to examine our images of God for their influence on our self-esteem. Before we can begin to experience the God of Abraham, Isaac, Jacob, and Jesus, we must destroy our whole pantheon of false gods and distorted images. We all have them. We have all burned incense at the shrines of our favorite gods. An all-time favorite god was portrayed several years ago in one of the main characters in the film *Cool Hand Luke.* In this film, prisoners put to work on the chain gang are governed by Boss Godfrey, an expressionless man who hides behind dark glasses. He never speaks, but he does carry a big stick and a rifle. Boss Godfrey has absolute power over the life and death of the men on the chain gang. The image of God that he portrays is that of a distant god who keeps book on us and waits for us to trip up so that we can be marked as a loser. This god threatens to imprison us in hell if we get out of line. If we perceive God like that, then surely we will have a hard time maintaining self-esteem.

But what if one's image of God were more like that played by George Burns in the film *Oh, God*? There we have a fun-loving old man joining in the affairs of life in such a delightful way. The self-esteem influenced by an image of a friendly, loving, close God would be more positive and the moral life less rigid than that supported by the image of a "gotcha" God and a perfectionistic moral life.

However, in our quest for self-esteem, we don't want to go to the extreme of denying any evil in ourselves. Common experience reminds us that our lives are a tangled web of good and evil. The uncanny insight of my five-year-old niece revealed this basic truth. I asked her once what color she would be if all good people in the world were painted blue and all the bad people were painted yellow. She thought for a moment and then matter of factly said, "I'd be streaky." She said what is true about us all. We are all streaky. There is some good in the worst of us and some evil in the best of us. In the depths of our hearts, we do battle with these conflicting tendencies. Because sin can be really within us and is really around us, we will never achieve total personal integration in this life. But we also believe that these dark forces are always encompassed by a greater power of good. This is the power of the unconditional love of God that sustains us and accepts us even when we feel unacceptable.

To deny or ignore our original blessing, to live with low or no self-esteem, only imprisons us in a defensive fear. Anger, resentment, jealousy, revenge, rivalry, and hoarding greed are all signs that we are deaf to the love that grounds us. Not sure that we are loved, we have to attack, put down, or dominate others in order to assure ourselves of the love we think we deserve.

Sin shows itself in our lives when we try to establish our worth on the basis of surrogate loves that we create to give us the security of being loveable and acceptable independent of God's love. These surrogate loves may be our talent, our goodness, our efficiency, our charm, our wit, our bright ideas, our wealth, our social position and prestige. But displacing divine love with these surrogate loves is nothing less than idolatry.

When we so fill up our lives with these idols of self-created loves, we have no room for divine love. The four blessings and the four woes of Luke (6:20–26) speak to this condition quite starkly. What is it about the poor, the hungry, the weeping and the rejected that they should receive a blessing, whereas those who are rich, filled, happy, and praised receive a curse? To be poor, hungry, weeping, and rejected are blessings of the reign of God because people in these conditions know they cannot establish themselves on any grounds of their own; rather, they rely totally on being supported by a love which comes to them out of its own abundance and not out of their own boasting or achievement. On the other hand, the rich, the filled, the happy, and the praised have no room in their lives for such love. They are filled already by their own achievements and, hanging on to these achievements as their sole source of security, are unable to surrender to divine love.

Not until we let go of these surrogate loves will we be free to surrender to the deepest truths about ourselves as being grounded in divine love. But letting go is hard. We hang on to these surrogate loves out of fear that if we let go we will lose our worth and no longer be valued or valuable. As long as we establish our worth in surrogate loves, we are not free. We remain trapped in the self-absorbing fear that believes that we are not loveable as we are. This fear and lack of freedom drives us to strive for qualities and achievements with which to exalt ourselves and oppress others. This only results in the self-righteousness that Jesus singles out as the obstacle to hearing the good news that our worth is grounded in God's love and not our own. We pronounce a judgment against ourselves when we refuse to accept this divine love as our only true source of worth and security. Not until we open ourselves to the source of our worth in God will we be open to the wider values of God's creation and God's people.

Strengthening Self-Esteem

To live the good life, we must accept our original blessing—God's love as the ground of our worth. Here is one of my favorite stories of accepting God's love. The old man in this story is well on his way to seeking the fulfillment of the good life because he knows that he is loved.

> One evening as the priest walked along the country road he came across an old man also out enjoying the twilight air. They walked and talked together until a sudden rain made them take shelter. When their conversation moved into silence, the old Irishman took his little prayer book and began praying half aloud. The priest watched him a long while, then in a quiet whisper said, "You must be very close to God!" The old man smiled very deeply and answered, "Yes! He is very fond of me!"[1]

Yes, God is very fond of us! More important, each of us needs to be able to say with this old man, "God is very fond of me!" But that may be our most difficult act of faith. It is indeed a great act of faith to believe that God is love. But it is an even greater act of faith to believe that God loves me! Why do we resist letting God love us? Is it that we do to

God what we do to others who say they love us? We want to know why. We tie their love to some quality we possess, some achievement we have done, some virtue we have acquired. We end up making their love another product we have produced. With God, we do not have to do anything as much as we have to stop doing things.

Perhaps many of us identify more easily with the peasant woman in *The Brothers Karamazov* than we do with this old man. In Dostoyevsky's novel, Father Zossima speaks these words to a penitent woman who could not let go of her sin and accept God's healing and liberating love:

> Fear nothing and never be afraid. And don't worry. If only your penitence fail not, God will forgive all. There is no sin, and there can be no sin on all the earth, which the Lord will not forgive to the truly repentant! Man cannot commit a sin so great as to exhaust the infinite love of God. Can there be a sin which could exceed the love of God? Think only of repentance, continual repentance, but dismiss fear altogether. Believe that God loves you as you cannot conceive; that He loves you with your sin, in your sin. It has been said of old that over one repentant sinner there is more joy in heaven than over ten righteous men. Go, and fear not. Be not bitter against men. Be not angry if you are wronged. Forgive the dead man in your heart what wrong he did you. Be reconciled with him in truth. If you are penitent, you love. And if you love you are of God. All things are atoned for, all things are saved by love. If I, a sinner even as you are, am tender with you and have pity on you, how much more will God have pity upon you. Love is such a priceless treasure that you can redeem the whole world by it, and cleanse not only your own sins but the sins of others.[2]

Father Zossima knew that repentance or accepting the gift of grace, of God's freely loving us, is the beginning of living the good life. God's love for us is the foundation on which the whole of the moral life rests. God loves us, all of us, without reservation. This is the basic fact of the moral life. We must never be willing to negotiate or compromise it. God never stops loving us. God loves us when we are in sin just as much as when we are out of sin. We cannot win God's love. We cannot lose God's love. But we are free to receive God's love or not. Even so, we could not even use this freedom unless God continued to love us. God is forever loving us. All we need to do is to live out of this love. Knowing that we are accepted by God and that God will never abandon us gives us unending courage to live morally day by day in friendship with God and with one another.

We all need to find ways to assimilate and reinforce this fundamental biblical insight about God's love for us. The scriptures never tire of repeating the word of God's love. The prophets extol God's love; Jesus lived by the truth of this word; and St. Paul spoke about its truth out of the depth of his experience. It is helpful for building self-esteem to develop the discipline of meditating on positive biblical stories and images that help us to understand divine love as our true source of worth and our only security. For example, try these. Listen to God say, "I love you":

Do not be afraid....I have called you by name—you are mine....You are precious to me....I love you....Do not be afraid—I am with you (Is 43:1–5).

Even if a mother should forget her child, I will never forget you....I have written your name in the palms of my hands (Is 49:15–16).

How can I give you up? How can I abandon you?...My heart will not let me do it! My love for you is too strong....I, the Holy One, am with you (Hos 11:8–9).

I love you just as the Father loves me; remain in my love (Jn 15:9).

For I am certain that nothing can separate us from his love: neither death nor life, neither angels nor other heavenly rulers or powers, neither the present nor the future, neither the world above nor the world below—there is nothing in all creation that will ever be able to separate us from the love of God which is ours through Christ Jesus our Lord (Rom 8:38–39).

If we are deaf to these words of love, then the burdens of self-doubt about our worth may overwhelm us and the hunger of our hearts to know that we count in the eyes of someone special may never be ultimately satisfied.

Spiritual Exercises

◆ In a quiet place, repeat the title of this chapter, "I have called you by name; you are precious to me," as your mantra, or breath prayer. Rest with this for a moment.

◆ Slowly read the scripture texts listed at the end of the chapter. Listen to God say, "I love you."

◆ So much of who we are is the handiwork of friends. Who are the people who have had the greatest influence on you? Recall your concentric circles from the last chapter? What names have those on the innermost circle given you? (For example, the family of a friend of mine has given her the name Sunshine because of how she lights up their life.) Let these names come. Spend time with them. Speak the names softly. What feelings accompany each name? What is the central conviction each name holds for you?

◆ Notice the kind of people you have in the innermost circles. What do they have that you would like to have? What makes you think that you do not already have it? What advantage would you have for being like them? What disadvantage are you suffering for not being like them?

◆ We all have had some experience that we regard as a mistake or even a failure. These can bruise our self-esteem. Reimagine that experience. Allow God to talk to you about it.

◆ Accepting God's love for us is the foundation of the good life. What images of God have you held that blocked you from accepting God's love? What images of God are liberating for you? Perhaps you may want to draw your image of God. What biblical story best expresses your image of God? Pray with that text slowly. This chapter includes lyrics from a song. Do you have a song or poem that expresses your experience or hope of love? Sing it, play it, or read it to your sharing group.

3.

I Will Be Your God, and You Will Be My People

The following story, "The Old Grandfather and the Grandson," by Leo Tolstoy raises some important questions about the good life:

The grandfather had become very old. His legs wouldn't go, his eyes didn't see, his ears didn't hear, he had no teeth. And when he ate, the food dripped from his mouth.

The son and daughter-in-law stopped setting a place for him at the table and gave him supper in back of the stove. Once they brought dinner down to him in a cup. The old man wanted to move the cup and dropped and broke it. The daughter-in-law began to grumble at the old man for spoiling everything in the house and breaking the cups and said that she would now give him dinner in a dishpan. The old man only sighed and said nothing.

Once the husband and wife were staying at home and watching their small son playing on the floor with some wooden planks: he was building something. The father asked: "What is that you are doing, Misha?" And Misha said: "Dear Father, I am making a dishpan. So that when you and dear Mother become old, you may be fed from this dishpan."

The husband and wife looked at one another and began to weep. They became ashamed of so offending the old man, and from then on seated him at the table and waited on him.[1]

What is your reaction to this story? How does it strike you? What feelings does it arouse in you? What does the story mean to you? With whom do you identify? Can you recall any events in your life when you were so preoccupied with your own interests that you failed to respond to a person in need? How might you behave differently in this situation if you were the grandfather, the son, the daughter-in-law, or Misha?

The last chapter reflected on some implications for the good life of the experience of covenantal love that establishes our worth and nurtures our self-esteem. This chapter is concerned with how the same covenantal love cultivates a moral character marked by the virtues of justice and solidarity. Because the covenant is all-inclusive, we have no other way of relating to God except in and through our relationships with everyone and everything else.

Tolstoy's story at the head of this chapter challenges our capacity for the virtue of solidarity and its work of love and justice. The story also evokes empathy and imagination inviting us to do as Atticus Finch advises in *To Kill a Mockingbird*: "Climb into someone else's skin and walk around in it awhile." It is this imaginative ability to share in someone else's feelings, ideas, or experiences, to understand their motivations, thoughts, or fears almost as if they were our own that affects our ability to act with love and justice. A capacity for empathy and imagination is necessary if we are ever to live the good life. We cannot be moral persons until we learn to appreciate what is not ourself. We could not live as covenantal partners bonded to one another and to God except through an affective grasp of the dignity of persons and the web of relationships that bonds us to one another and to the environment.

In an imaginative way, the story evokes some very familiar covenantal images from the Bible. One is the prophetic image of God giving us new hearts of flesh to replace our stony hearts:

> I will give them a new heart, and put a new spirit within them; I will remove the heart of stone from their flesh and give them a heart of flesh, so that they may follow my statutes and keep my ordinances and obey them. Then they shall be my people, and I will be their God. (Ez 11:19–20)

Another is the familiar Golden Rule—do to others as you would have them do to you—and the great commandment of Jesus—love God above all and your neighbor as yourself—which is a moral imperative of the reign of God proclaimed by Jesus. Variations of the phrase "I will be your God, and you will be my people" are frequently repeated by the prophets as a shorthand summary of the covenant reminding Israel that God wants to form one people who would be bonded to one another and to God as one community of friends.

The insight of the covenant is that we are an interdependent community where individual good is bound up with the good of the whole. Without community we wither. This stands in stark contrast to the liberal forces of our culture that take independence and separation as the norm. But according to the covenant, this is to have it all backwards. The dominant ethic of American individualism understands the person in terms of *I, me,* or *mine.* It extols society as a loose association of individuals who stand side by side, bound together by self-interest. The covenant, by contrast, understands personal existence only in terms of the connections that make for communal existence. Thus, there is no sharp distinction between private and public spheres because we are one interdependent community with others, with the Earth, and with God. This relational understanding of the self has some wide-ranging implications for the moral form of the good life. At its center is a fundamental commitment to justice, to restoring right relationships.

Justice

In the Bible, when justice is ignored, the prophets cry out that the covenant is broken. Something is wrong in the relation between society and its members. Something is wrong in their relation to God. In the absence of justice, acts of pious devotion are repugnant to God. The prophet Amos makes a strong indictment of religion without justice:

> I hate, I despise your festivals,
>> and I take no delight in your solemn assemblies.
> Even though you offer me your burnt offerings and
>> grain offerings,
>> I will not accept them;
>> and the offerings of well-being of your fatted animals
>> I will not look upon.
> Take away from me the noise of your songs;
>> I will not listen to the melody of your harps.
> But let justice roll down like waters,
>> and righteousness like an ever flowing stream.
>> (Am 5:21–24)

The imagery is striking. By comparing justice and righteousness with flowing water, Amos shows that without justice there can be no life in the land.

Biblical justice is hard for us to grasp. It is so different from what we know as U.S. justice. In Washington D.C. stands the symbol of U.S. justice—a blindfolded woman holding balanced scales. Notice the imagery. Balanced scales suggest arithmetic equality. The blindness suggests that the judicial decision is not concerned with the person affected by the judgment but only with the reality being judged. When we put this image of justice as impartial and equal alongside the Bible, we can only be struck by the illogic of God. U.S. justice focuses on fairness in procedures and equality in outcomes irrespective of the person. It cuts the pie into equal pieces. It keeps a ledger where accounts are squared. Such a stripped-down version of justice may well define the minimal standards of regulating the exchange between individuals, but it does not pay attention to the social character of justice. As a result, we tend to equate justice with protecting personal freedoms and so reduce justice to the work of the courts that punish those who harm us. We feel that justice is done when retribution is made. We are blinded, however, to the larger duty we have to the common good, to the social ties that bind us to one another, especially to the weakest in our societies, and to the kind of structures we need to create in order to sustain a healthy community.

Biblical justice, by contrast, keeps no ledger. It takes the blindfold off. It sees who is tampering with the scales because biblical justice knows that the scales don't balance. Instead of scales and an impartial blindfold, biblical justice passionately expresses the causes of the poor and needy. In the imagery of the prophets, justice is like a mighty mountain river, roaring down a ravine with enormous power, taking with it everything it touches and sweeping away all inequities.

From these biblical roots, an understanding of justice has continued to evolve and grow through the Christian tradition. Three of its themes have been characteristic of the Catholic justice tradition:

1. *Human Dignity*

The dignity of each person is a gift of God. It does not depend on race, sex, economic status, or human achievement. Human dignity is rooted in being made in the image of God. The church bases its teachings about justice on this fundamental belief in the sacredness of the human person. The previous chapters have already explored some of the implications for the good life of resting dignity on being made in the image of God.

2. *The Common Good*

The human person is not only sacred but also social. The human person is defined relationally—by the relationships he or she has with God, other persons, and other creatures. The command of Jesus to love your neighbor has an individual dimension, to be sure. But it also entails a broader social commitment. We are all, in a spiritual sense, sisters and brothers to one another. The good of each person is bound up with the good of other persons and other creatures. Justice requires that everyone have an opportunity to share in the basic goods necessary for participation in the human community.

The common good is the term used in the Catholic tradition to convey the well-being that we strive to achieve by living in solidarity with and for one another. The common good is not the sum total of individual goods, nor is it the good of the majority taking precedence over individual rights. While it respects and serves the interests of individual persons, the common good ultimately upholds the good of society as a whole to be more important than the good of any one individual. It believes that the individual will flourish only insofar as society as a whole flourishes. A commitment to the common good forces us to ask whether there are some things that we want for ourselves but which we ought not to pursue so that the good of the whole might be better served. The dynamic of giving and receiving that was the theme of the first chapter is the very dynamic of this communitarian perspective which wants to protect an individual's good while securing the well-being of others. In short, the common good keeps the best interests of the individual and the well-being of the community as a whole in tension. Its achievement depends on the generosity and commitment of individuals and institutions to seek those actions and policies that will provide for the good of the individual as well as for the good of others.

3. *Concern for the Poor*

The biblical test of the character of any society is its treatment of the poor. But who are the poor? They are anyone whose dignity is on the line. Anyone who has walked the streets of any American city readily recognizes them as the ones lacking material goods of food, clothing, and shelter like Lazarus in the Lukan parable (Lk 16:19–31). However, the poor are also those who have no voice to advocate on their own and so are powerless to influence public policies. One of the striking features of this Lukan parable is that the rich man has no name, but he does have a strong voice to advocate his cause. Lazarus, by contrast, has a name by which he can be identified, but he has no voice with which to be heard.

The substance of our covenantal commitment is to see that the poor have basic material resources as well as a voice so that they can defend themselves and not be excluded from social life, the market place, or the workforce. If we forget the poor, we are forgetting a truth about ourselves implied in our radical interconnectedness to God and to one another revealed in the covenantal expression "I will be your God, and you will be my people." The prophets, most explicitly Amos, Isaiah, and Jeremiah, protested that because the hungry were not fed, the poor left homeless, and the orphans not cared for, Israel had forgotten who they were as covenantal partners with God and with one another. The prophets spoke not only on behalf of God, but also on behalf of those who had no voice.

Two of the strongest prophetic texts affirming that faith in our covenantal God involves doing justice are from Jeremiah and Isaiah. In these texts, true religion—knowing God and praising God in religious ritual—is equated with doing justice, with taking up the causes of the poor and the needy. Note Jeremiah's word to the king:

> Thus says the Lord: Act with justice and righteousness, and deliver from the hand of the oppressor anyone who has been robbed. And do no wrong or violence to the alien, the orphan, and the widow, or shed innocent blood in this place.
> Woe to him who builds his house by
>   unrighteousness,
> and his upper rooms by injustice.
> Did not your father eat and drink
> and do justice and righteousness?
> Then it was well with him.
> He judged the cause of the poor and needy;
> then it was well.
> Is this not to know me?
>   says the Lord. (Jer 22:3, 13, 15–16)

In the vision of Isaiah, true religion requires not the reforming of rituals but the reforming of lives so that justice may be done:

> Is such the fast that I choose, a day to humble oneself?
> Is it to bow down the head like a bulrush,

and to lie in sackcloth and ashes?
Will you call this a fast, a day acceptable to the Lord?
Is this not the fast that I choose:
    to loose the bonds of injustice,
    to undo the thongs of the yoke,
    to let the oppressed go free,
    and to break every yoke?
Is it not to share your bread with the hungry,
    and bring the homeless poor into your house;
    when you see the naked, to cover them,
    and not to hide yourself from your own kin?
Then your light shall break forth like the dawn,
    and your healing shall spring up quickly;
    your vindicator shall go before you,
    the glory of the Lord shall be your rear guard.
Then you shall call, and the Lord will answer;
    you shall cry for help, and he will say, Here I am.
                                    (Is 58:5–9)

These two texts, along with that of Amos above, affirm that we cannot be just and religious if we do not heed God's call to take the cause and defend the rights of the poor and oppressed in the community.

Why are we to stand with the poor? Very simply, because God does. As partners in the covenant, we are to value what God values. Human justice is to reflect divine justice. For the good life, being friends with God also includes befriending all that God loves as well. When God took the side of the oppressed Hebrew slaves in Egypt, delivered them to safety, and lived among them, God was showing that their suffering and hopes were God's very own. The prophets frequently had to remind the chosen people that the quality of their faith depended on the character of justice, and the character of justice was tested by how the oppressed and the outcast—"the widow, the orphan, and the stranger"—fared among them.

The dominant theme of the preaching and teaching of Jesus is the reign of God, a new order of justice and peace guided by the great commandment to love God and neighbor as yourself. What Jesus proclaimed in word, he also enacted. In the ministry of Jesus, we see God revealing a love for "the lost, the least, and the last" over and over again. Jesus reached out to women and those considered outcasts, he took up the cause of those who suffered religious and social discrimination, he crossed the line between Jews and Samaritans, he reached out to Gentiles, he welcomed children, he showed mercy to sinners. Luke's Jesus echoes Isaiah to say something about how we are to live together in covenant when he proclaims in his inaugural sermon, "I have come to bring good news to the poor, to proclaim liberty to captives, recovery of sight to the blind, freedom to prisoners, and to announce a year of favor from the Lord" (Lk 4:18). Matthew's Jesus not only makes clear that we are to care for the poor but that we are to be identified with the poor as Jesus is. The last judgment scene in the parable of the sheep and the goats tells us that Jesus, who came as Emmanuel (God with us), so identifies with the poor as to lie hidden in our midst, wrapping himself in those most in need—the hungry, the naked, the homeless, the sick and imprisoned. What we do to these, we do to Jesus (Mt 25: 31–46). The parable, in effect, says that our judgment lies in how we stand with the poor and how we do corporal works of mercy for those in need. To reject the poor is to reject God manifest in them.

Solidarity

How do we stand with the poor? In one of the major documents of the Second Vatican Council, "The Church in the Modern World," the church expressed in an unprecedented way its solidarity with the entire human family. Here is the opening sentence:

> The joys and the hopes, the griefs and the anxieties of men and women of this age, especially of those who are poor or in any way afflicted, these too are the joys and hopes, the griefs and anxieties of the followers of Christ.

In this document, the church defined itself as a church for others. Its task is to bear the burden with other people, to struggle with others for justice, and to strengthen the bonds that unite people despite their differences. So when it comes to standing with the poor in solidarity, with our economic, social, and political structures, we cannot check our faith at the door. How we express ourselves reflects whether we truly believe that we are covenantal partners participating in the reign of God. The letter of James has a strong statement about putting our faith into action:

> What good is it, my brothers and sisters, if you say you have faith but do not have works? Can faith save you? If a brother or sister is naked and lacks daily food, and one of you says to them, "Go in peace; keep warm and eat your fill," and yet you do not supply their bodily needs, what is the good of that? So faith by itself, if it has no works, is dead. (Jas 2:14–17)

The virtue of solidarity disposes us toward covenantal interdependence and standing with the poor. Pope John Paul II spoke of solidarity as a virtue in his social encyclical, *Sollicitudo Rei Socialis* (December 30, 1987):

> [Solidarity] then is not a feeling of vague compassion or shallow distress at the misfortunes of so many people, both near and far. On the contrary, it is a firm and persevering determination to commit oneself to the common good; that

is to say to the good of all and of each individual because we are all really responsible for all. (n. 38)

The covenant is not fully realized until we live out the covenantal commitment to be responsible to and for one another as covenantal partners. The covenantal laws express the responsibility we have to and for one another by virtue of our sharing in the same divine love. This is the core of the inseparability of the great commandment to love God and others as we love ourself. The great commandment requires that each of us recognize that the other matters for his or her own sake and not just as the means to an end.

Standing with the poor in solidarity can occur in three movements—seeing, judging, and acting.[2] First, we must begin to *see differently*. As a virtue, solidarity helps us to see others, not for how we can use them to serve our own interests and then discard them when they are no longer useful, but as partners with us, sharing our humanity. While it is always right to begin by meeting our responsibilities to those nearest us, our vision and interest must become increasingly global. An ancient rabbi had a saying that gives us an image for the person of expansive vision and interest. "He who cares for his own child is like a stream which nourishes a tree along its banks. But he who loves another's child is like a cloud which goes from the sea into the desert and waters there a lonesome tree."

When God inquired after the missing Abel, Cain gave the surly response, "Am I my brother's keeper?" (Gn 4:9). His question was a way of refusing to accept the responsibility that everyone has toward others. Cain's question makes us think of our refusal to reach beyond our inner circle to include society's weakest members—children, the elderly, immigrants—and to be indifferent toward relations between peoples even when basic values such as survival, freedom, or peace are at stake. But we can no longer limit our caring to those in our own family. We must include the whole human family. We are all our "brother's keeper" for God has entrusted each of us to one another.

When Jesus challenged his disciples to "love your neighbor as yourself," he was asked, "And who is my neighbor?" (Lk 10:29). In response he told the story of the Samaritan who interrupted his journey and went out of his way to see that the man he found beaten and lying in the ditch would get whatever he needed to be restored to health. The force of the story lies in the fact that these two men were not only complete strangers to each other but that Jews and Samaritans at that time were mortal enemies. So there was no expectation of loyalty or special obligation toward each other. The Samaritan, however, does not respond to the Jew as an enemy but as a friend in need. In this way, the story shows that to be neighbor one does not have to be someone to whom we have made a special commitment. Neighbors are anyone in need. They are not only those for whom we choose to care, but they are also those whom we have not chosen but are given to us—the poor, the rejected, those who are unable to provide for themselves. All members of the human community, even enemies, are given over to each other's care.

Living in the global village as we do makes it imperative that we see everyone as neighbor. An ancient rabbi asked his students how they could tell when night had ended and day was on its way back. "Could it be when you see an animal in the distance and can tell whether it is a sheep or a dog?" "No," answered the rabbi. "Could it be when you look at a tree in the distance and can tell whether it is a fig tree or a peach tree?" "No." "Well, then," demanded the students, "when is it?" "It is when you look on the face of any woman or man and see that she or he is your sister or brother. Because if you can't do that, then no matter what time it is, it is still night for you."

To look into the face of any other and to see a sister or brother is the seeing of empathy. It is seeing with the heart. As in Leo Tolstoy's story of the grandfather and the grandson, such seeing often requires firsthand experience of the marginalized and disadvantaged. Empathy takes time. But not until we move out of ourselves and into the experience of another, will we ever act differently towards them. Atticus Finch was right. We will never really know another until we stand in their shoes and walk around in them. When we come to know poor persons, people whose lives are filled with joy and sorrow, love and hope, success and failure like our own, then we are less likely to tolerate racial, ethnic, political, or sexist discrimination against them. The seeing of empathy can open us to a new vision, a "structural vision," that sees beyond individual human need to the social structures that must be changed if the human need is ever to be addressed adequately.

Second, once we begin to see differently, we must begin to *judge differently.* Our lives extend beyond a private relationship with God and our neighbor to embrace the whole social order—social structures, institutional order, economic systems. Our lives are inevitably marked by the structural relationships that can act for or against an individual's rights and the common good. We are more connected today in terms of communication, transportation, economic, political, and environmental structures and interests than ever before. Domestic economic issues have implications on foreign markets; environmental carelessness in one region has an impact on the ecosystem across those regional boundaries. Our interconnectedness in the choices we make and in the deeds we do is well illustrated humorously, but pointedly, in this incident: Three men go rowing together in one boat. One begins to drill a hole in the boat underneath his seat. The other two panic and scream to him in their fear, "What do you think you're doing?" With calm detachment, he answers, "What is it to you? I am only making the hole under my own seat."

When making plans or setting up a new social or economic structure, an important question to ask from the perspective of the virtue of solidarity is the following: "How will this impact the poor and disadvantaged?" For a simple illustration, consider this example. Picture a loaf of bread in the middle of a table. Around the table are people of different ages, ethnic backgrounds, nations, abilities, and socioeconomic status. The bread is to be divided among them. What is the most just way to do this? The American sense of justice would say that the loaf of bread should be divided equally. The biblical sense of justice would find out who is most in need and then would divide the loaf so that the neediest received more. Biblical justice focuses more on needs for individuals and the common good than it does on fair procedures and merely equal distribution.

From this perspective, the U.S. bishops, in their pastoral letter *Economic Justice for All* (1986), say that we ought to keep three concerns before us when making plans and distributing resources: "Decisions must be judged in light of what they do *for* the poor, what they do *to* the poor, and what they enable the poor to do *for themselves*" (n. 24). Questions such as these challenge us not to take for granted the way things are but to look with critical suspicion for how decisions and structures are at the service of all people, but especially the poor.

The third movement in exercising the virtue of solidarity is to *act differently*. In the face of so much need, and the vast number of poor, we ask "What can I do?" We feel powerless before the enormity of poverty and the extent of misery. The Canadian Catholic bishops have presented a five-step process that takes us from standing with the poor to acting in solidarity with them:

- to attend to the experience of the poor,
- to analyze the structures that cause suffering,
- to judge values and priorities in light of the gospel,
- to imagine alternative models for social development,
- to act in solidarity with those struggling to transform society.[3]

On a less grand scale, we can begin by sowing seeds. We begin small by learning to approach questions from the perspective of justice and by acquiring an understanding of and respect for other cultures and ethnic groups, by becoming familiar with the social dynamics of prejudice and its consequences and with the structural causes and effects of poverty and economic insecurity. We can be sensitive to the use of inclusive language and to avoiding racist or sexist slurs. We can monitor our own purchasing practice and investments to see whether we are supporting corporations that have policies that advance the cause of the poor. We can also be mindful of our own overall consumption of goods and the accumulation of possessions. Small steps such as these may not effect great change in the world, but they can have a great effect on us. Who we are deep down spills over into our lives. What we do over time makes us who we are. In the good life we want to become more just and more in solidarity with all, especially the poor.

The Environment

God's covenantal love in the broadest sense is not limited just to humanity but is directed also toward all creation. We who consciously accept this covenant with God accept responsibility for all of creation as well. The covenant teaches us the same lesson that we are learning through our scientific explorations—namely, that every facet of the universe is bound together by an unbreakable bond of relatedness. A quote from John Muir inscribed on a metal placard at the beginning of a trail in Yosemite National Park reminds us of this truth: "When we try to pick out something by itself, we find it hitched to everything else in the universe." In short, nothing exists by itself as an independent entity. Everything exists in dynamic interrelationship. This is true not only for us but also for everything else in creation.

Part of our covenantal responsibility is to be in solidarity with all creation. We exercise the virtue of solidarity toward the environment by being good stewards of creation. For too long we humans have acted as if we are the reason that everything else exists. Relating to creation this way is much like spoiled, self-centered children on the playground who want everyone else to play with them and only them and, of course, by their own rules.

We are at a point today where we must see and judge our relation to creation differently. We must begin to see the cosmos as an ecosystem to which we belong rather than as a planet placed here for us to use at will. Issues of clean air and water, toxic wastes, diminishing natural resources, ravaged rain forests, endangered species, and populations are not artificial problems. They are real. It is time that we live consciously in harmony with nature rather than continue to assume dominion over it. We must begin to ask what our policies and practices are doing to the environment and for the environment. Recycling, conservation, and an ecosensitive lifestyle can reflect our solidarity with the environment and responsibility to it and for it.

Throughout life we have the opportunity to better our world. When we live with indifference, jealously, envy, contempt, domination, possessiveness, greed, or prejudice and ignore situations of need requiring works of justice, mercy, and love, then we are failing to heed the covenantal summons of divine-human solidarity. In so doing, we pronounce a judgment against ourselves. Our obligations inherent in being covenantal partners are inseparable from the bond that links us to God. The great index of the good life is that we stand on the side of the poor and champion the rights of those least able to fend for or defend themselves. In this area we have some outstanding models of the virtues of justice and solidarity in Francis and Clare, Vincent de Paul, Dorothy Day, Martin Luther King, Jr., and Mother Teresa. They have shown us how human solidarity is one piece with our relationship to God. To betray a social or environmental commitment demanded by justice and solidarity is to betray God.

Spiritual Exercises

◆ In a quiet place, repeat the title of this chapter, "I will be your God, and you will be my people," as a mantra or breath prayer. Rest with this for a moment.

◆ Read again Leo Tolstoy's short story at the head of the chapter. What feelings does it arouse in you? Share your reaction to this story with a friend. Take on the role of each of the characters, and feel what this event is like from their perspective.

◆ Follow the evening news for a week. Watch for ways U.S. justice tries to balance the ledger. How would an appeal to biblical justice, which is passionately inclusive and committed to the poor and needy, change the way some newsworthy events would turn out?

◆ Take one of the popular news magazines and identify the "widows, orphans, and strangers" of today. How does your image of the poor affect the way you think about justice? If you do this exercise in a group, you might make a collage of the pictures that you take from the magazines.

◆ Solidarity with all creation is integral to our covenantal relationships. Take a walk through the woods, in the park, along the shore. Take your shoes off. Feel the earth. Bring home a symbol that will remind you of your connection to the earth. In how many ways can we be more careful about promoting harmony with the earth? Brainstorm some "good earth" strategies.

4.

I Desire Faithfulness, Not Sacrifice

Remember the trust walk—a common exercise on many youth retreats? Two people would pair up. One would be blindfolded and then led through unknown territory by the other as a guide. When blindfolded, they had to trust that they would not be led into anything that would harm them. The exercise was simple, the experience memorable, and the message profound. The exercise was designed to touch the very basic disposition that makes a religious response possible in the first place—trust. The other would act as a guide embodying what it is like to be a faithful imitator of the God whom we trust will not betray us. Fidelity to trust weaves the fabric of a covenantal relationship. Without it, everything falls apart.

The solidarity of covenantal partners who have responsibility to and for one another needs fidelity or trustworthiness in order to come to its fullest expression. The prophets reminded Israel that this faithfulness is at the heart of the covenant: "What I want is faithfulness, not sacrifice" (Hos 6:6). This chapter will explore faithfulness and its related virtues—fidelity, loyalty, and trustworthiness—as further characteristics of our life together in a covenantal community.

Covenantal Faithfulness

In the promissory covenant with Noah (Gn 9:8–17), with Abraham (Gn 15 and 17), and with David (2 Sm 7), the promise of loyalty is in one direction. In the Sinai covenant, by contrast, the emphasis is less on God's loyalty and more on the demands of Israel to be loyal. This demand for absolute loyalty is the substance of the first commandment.

When the people of Israel turn away from God and no longer heed their covenantal responsibilities, God sends prophets to call them back to their covenantal commitment. The prophets declare God's faithfulness while interpreting the covenantal demands to return to fidelity and not to rely on their ritual sacrifices to satisfy their covenantal commitment. The prophets show that God continues to be faithful by supporting the covenant even in the face of infidelity. In Hosea, for example, God is faithful in spite of Israel's infidelity (Hos 11). In the New Testament, God's promise of loyalty is in Jesus who is described as "the son of David, the son of Abraham" (Mt 1:1). The very title, Christ, also witnesses to Jesus' being the promised one of God, the Messiah, who fulfills all the hopes of the covenant.

The history of Israel shows how their fidelity to God was sorely threatened when the people asked for a king like the other nations. To turn from a tribal federation under the sovereignty of God to a monarchy under a king was a serious theological problem for them. To whom would Israel ultimately be loyal, the God of the covenant or the king?

Gideon is portrayed as a man who would *not* be king because only God is the ruler of Israel. An earthly king would be in constant conflict with the sovereignty of God and threaten the single-hearted loyalty that the covenant commanded. Making a king raised the issue of infidelity and idolatry all over again. The first commandment of the covenant already forbade that. Earthly leaders can become like gods and displace the loyalty only God deserves.

The theological problem of divine sovereignty is resolved for Israel by having the king appointed by God through a prophet (1 Sm 8). If anyone would be king, then he is to be appointed by God. The ideal king is the one who will rule with all the qualities of God's justice, and so we get the dynasty of David from whose house came Jesus proclaiming the reign of God.

Faithful Belonging

The Old Testament story of the rise of the monarchy and the subsequent stories of the prophets who constantly reminded the kings and the people that God was the one to whom they were ultimately loyal challenge us today when we are tempted to idolatry and compromises of loyalty. We all live with the tension of having so many claims made on our loyalty—everything from family and friends to political parties, ethnic groups to church groups, social clubs to ball clubs. In the midst of so many demands on our hearts, where do we find our center, that single focus that gives direction to our lives? The diverse claims made on us can easily give us the impression that all claims are of equal value. In the midst of such diversity, where are we going to root ourselves so that we can find a clear perspective or a single focus that gives direction to our lives?

We all know from our efforts to raise a garden or even to

plant a window box of herbs or flowers that the best way for anything to grow is to put down roots. In covenantal relationships, to put down roots is to be faithful. A scene from *Butterflies Are Free* illustrates this well. The covenantal relationship in that story is between a young girl and her blind lover. When she decides to run away from him, her reason is that "you are blind; you are crippled." The young man replies, "No, I am not crippled. I am sightless but not crippled. You are crippled because you can't commit yourself to anyone. You can't belong." Faithfulness that puts down roots is to belong. If we don't know how to be faithful, we don't know how to belong in a way that enables each to live together in a way that enables everyone to flourish.

A powerful scene from Arthur Miller's *The Misfits* captures well the pain of not being able to belong. Rosalind and her husband have decided to break up their marriage, but he doesn't want her to move out of the house completely. He invites his wife to continue to live on in the house but to go their separate ways. She says in response to his invitation, "If I am going to have to live alone, I would rather do it all by myself." Faithfulness is what is required if we are ever to grow together as covenantal partners.

Betrayal of Trust

Where one cannot trust another to be loyal to the covenantal commitment, the relationship of love breaks down. One of the most bitter moments in the lives of those who join in covenant is to find out that the one we believed had been committed to us is not being faithful to that commitment. Such moments arouse our moral indignation at the betrayal of trust.

In the story of Jesus and his disciples, after the foot

washing scene in the gospel of John (13:1–20), we hear Jesus expressing with troubled spirit that he is going to be betrayed. After taking the piece of bread that Jesus offers him, Judas immediately goes out into the night. Why does this brief reference to Judas occur in a scene dominated by Jesus' giving an example of servanthood? What could the gospel writer want to communicate by giving attention to Judas? In the context of a fellowship meal, Judas underscores the shame of betrayal and demonstrates by contrast the trustworthiness in those who follow Christ. Trustworthiness is central to what it means to be an image of God's covenantal faithfulness.

How would you feel if someone were to violate a confidence, to deceive you so as to enhance his or her self-interest, or to lie about you to another so as to ruin your life? I suspect *betrayed* is the word that best describes your feeling. When we experience such betrayal, we sometimes hedge against any future infidelity by defending ourselves against the forces of an imbalance of power. This infects all our relationships with the suspicion and the fear that fidelity is not being practiced in our commitments to one another. Betrayal captures this violation of trust. Judas was called to embody the covenantal fidelity that God has with all of us, but he proved to be untrustworthy. In violating a trust, we are not only doing the wrong thing, but we are becoming the wrong kind of person. We are becoming a betrayer like Judas, violating the command to follow Jesus in imitating God's fidelity.

Trustworthiness

The trustworthiness that is characteristic of the good life is not only a trust that God's gracious acceptance of us is something that we can rely on, but it is also a trust that God trusts us. God has entrusted us with creation, with each other, and with many gifts that enable us to live in covenant together in ways that will enhance the well-being of all. The challenge to trust in the good life is to know oneself as entrusted with many gifts and to draw out the trustworthiness of others by encouraging them to be all that they can be.

We see the virtue of trustworthiness or fidelity played out in the contrast of two garden stories in the Bible, the garden of Eden (Gn 2—3) and the garden of Gethsemane (Mt 26).[1] Both can be seen as stories of what we do with our freedom to live as trustworthy partners in covenant.

On the sixth day of creation, God entrusted the earth to the care of Adam and Eve, placed them in the garden to cultivate it, and entrusted them to each other. The story implies that everything comes to us as a gift from a free and gracious God. The story of the garden of Eden is pervaded with the sense that humanity is empowered with the capacity to influence creation and one another by being entrusted with gifts, the gifts of creation and the gifts of one another. Yet into that ideal setting, the serpent enters to sow seeds of distrust. The serpent suggests to the man and the woman that God cannot be trusted and so tempts the creatures with power (the knowledge of good and evil). Adam and Eve choose to believe the snake. In this, they miss the mark of remaining loyal to the covenantal relationship. With their fall they admit into the world alienation, betrayal, twisted motives, and the need to build protective defenses that keep others out and that keep the self secure. By distrusting God, Adam and Eve reverse their basic relationship to life. When dwelling within God's trust and returning that trust, they centered themselves on God as the source and support of their fulfillment. Now that they dwell in distrust, they settle within themselves. They move from centering their ultimate loyalty on God to being idolatrously self-centered. This is the root of sin—to have an excessive preference of self over others.

The moment they refuse to believe that God can be trusted, when they betray their covenantal commitment, Adam and Eve refuse to trust each other also. They imprison themselves within their own fear and defenses. The freedom that they knew when in a trusting relationship with God would not have shrunk from the demands of relationships, sexuality, friendships, and social responsibility. However, the fear of distrust does. The fear of distrust becomes suspicious of all relationships. Fear builds walls of protection, and seeks the control of domination and the power of manipulation.

When Adam and Eve become estranged from God, they become estranged from each other also. Now separation, suspicion, and fear become the marks of their lives. This is symbolized by their hiding in the bushes to protect themselves from God and by their sewing fig leaves for clothes to hide their nakedness and so protect themselves from one another. To stand naked before another is to leave oneself vulnerable. It says to the other, "I trust you. I am willing to hand myself over to you. I am ready to risk all that I am with you." Adam and Eve could no longer allow themselves to be that vulnerable. From this point, all of life becomes marked by the suspicion of betrayal and by walls of protection that hedge against infidelity and other abuses of power.

The story of the garden of Gethsemane, on the other hand, is the story of Jesus trusting in God by not abandoning his mission of living to make everyone a friend of God and of one another. This garden story brings us back from the fear that tells us not to trust—not to trust God, not to trust anyone. Whereas Adam and Eve used their freedom to become strangers, Jesus used his to make friends. Jesus lived for the sake of making everyone a friend of God and of one another. Jesus showed that his relationship with the Father was one of loyal trust by enabling others to recognize that they too had been entrusted by God with precious gifts and by providing them with a safe space of acceptance wherein they might trust themselves to share the gifts entrusted to them. Jesus' great act of living by covenantal fidelity was to accept death on the cross, trusting that his life would not evaporate into an empty future. Jesus lived his life trusting that he would be sustained by the undefeatable love of God. The resurrection confirms that such trust was vindicated.

In the story of the garden of Gethsemane, Judas again appears as an important figure for understanding covenantal fidelity. His betrayal of Jesus with a kiss contrasts with God's faithfulness to Jesus and Jesus' fidelity to God. With Judas in the story, we see more clearly the centrality of fidelity in the lives of those who covenant with Jesus as disciples. To violate fidelity is to violate the call to follow Jesus in the imitation of God's covenantal, steadfast love.

The stories of the garden of Eden and the garden of Gethsemane teach us that we are pursued by the relentless fidelity of God. Sin is the power play of infidelity. Sin is refusing to believe that God can be trusted and that others, and even ourselves, are worth trusting. In a covenant, we entrust to one another something of value to ourselves. In God's covenant with humanity, for example, God has entrusted to us divine love, most fully expressed in the person of Jesus. In marriage we covenant with another by entrusting to another our whole selves and our lives. This is symbolized in giving our bodies to each other. In health care, we covenant by entrusting our physical well-being to a health-care professional. In covenants with lawyers, we entrust our legal rights to a legal professional.

In making these acts of trust, we entrust the other with power over us. We hope that this power will not be abused.

Sin is the misuse of power by failing to hold in trust that which has been entrusted to us, such as a personal secret, our health, our property, our bodies. In sin we refuse to live in the freedom of being entrusted by God with personal worth and with the gifts of one another. Rather than living in trust as creatures empowered with gifts to set one another free, we live in suspicion of another's gifts and abuse our power by controlling, dominating, or manipulating these gifts to serve our own self-interests. Sin also misuses power when it fails to assume the responsibility we ought to assume to set relationships right between persons and communities. We sin whenever we distort by action or omission the mutual respect that should bind us together.

The Challenge to Trust

Trying to learn fidelity and trust is not easy. We find it hard to trust and to accept entrustment in the way covenantal friendship demands. We know our world is a rough place in which to live, so we are suspicious of give and take. We enjoy control; we count what we give so as to be sure to get back at least what we gave; we like to do things together as long as we're doing what we like to do. The place of trust and fidelity in the good life can be too easy and slick for the kind of world we know. Living in trust is not always contemplating the lilies of the field. Slick talk of trust recalls the hucksterism of P. T. Barnum: "There is a sucker born every minute and two to take him."

Are we to take the virtue of trust as a call to gullibility? No. Trust that is a virtue of the good life is not a call to some sort of romantic vision of a life that has no evil in it or to some form of destructive gullibility or a misplaced surrender. It is not a call to a passive handing over of responsibility either. Nor should trust be blind to the wholly untrustworthy and deceptive. While expecting not a rose garden but something more like the garden of Gethsemene, trust simply does not allow the forces of evil to dictate the terms of our relationships. Nonviolent resistance to evil is an example of this kind of trust. The trust that nonviolence attempts may appear foolish and unproductive; yet this is the kind of trust that distinguishes the good life as lived by Jesus.

The trust that is the virtue of the good life does not become disillusioned when it meets with untrustworthiness in the places we least expect to find it. Trust knows that our experiences are filled with ambiguity and that we act with a mix of motives. But trust holds the course in the direction of pursuing the good that is possible. As a virtue, it prizes those moments when trustworthiness is clearly the dominant part of experience. While prudently testing whatever and whoever claims to be trustworthy, trust refuses to become so suspicious as to be blind to anything or anyone worthy of trust.

Practicing Trust and Fidelity

To regard covenantal trust and fidelity as core virtues of the good life prepares us to engage in those practices that enable us to build bonds of friendship. In any household with more than one child, the parents often say, "Why can't you get along better with each other?" The parents' hope is that the children will acquire an appreciation for each other and become friends. To that end, parents try to teach their children how to enjoy one another's company. So they play games with them, take them on picnics, engage them in family chores, train them to understand the importance of give and take. Through practices like these, parents try to teach their children that living together in trust and fidelity can make for a richer life for everyone.

So if we want to be virtuous in the way trust and fidelity require, then we need to engage in practices that strengthen them: respect physical and emotional boundaries in a relationship; risk sharing happy or sad moments with a friend; respect what has been confided to us; honor others even in their absence; protect their best interests when in a position to do so; set aside some time to be together and then show up when we say we will be there; pay attention while together; stop measuring or counting what the other does or does not do; follow through on commitments and keep in touch—with phone calls, letters, or e-mail; cook more dinners and linger a little longer around the table; take more walks in the park. These are moral tasks of the good life. They are not just social niceties.

The stories of the two gardens teach us that we are pursued by the steadfast faithfulness of God. God's relentless trust in us never lets our fears and suspicions become so dark and deep that we fail to recognize that we have been entrusted by God. We are called to imitate God's fidelity by entrusting others and eliciting trust from them. We are free to trust others because we know that we have been entrusted by God and that we trust in God. If we can let go of fear and suspicion and come to see trust more as gift than as threat, then we will be able to answer to what is of God in the other. This is the way of the good life. It demands that our preliminary inclinations to fear and suspicion be repositioned in the direction of trust, trusting our own gifts and trusting the gifts of another. The daily effect of trusting and being trustworthy is to break through barriers of fear and to take a risk on our own goodness and on the goodness of another. What God has trusted we must start trusting. What God has been willing to take a risk on, we must be willing to take risks on. Only when someone gives us permission to start to trust ourselves (as God already has) will we take ourselves seriously with our gifts (as God already does). Only when we start to trust ourselves will we be able to take full responsibility for living the good life.

Spiritual Exercises

◆ In a quiet place, repeat the title of this chapter, "I desire faithfulness, not sacrifice," as a mantra or breath prayer. Rest with this for a moment.

◆ Reflect on your experiences of belonging—to another person, to a community, to a cause. What does it demand from you to belong? What do you need from others to make it possible to belong?

◆ Share a story of a betrayed trust—a confidence disclosed, a commitment broken, a vulnerability exploited. What feelings accompany the experience you are recalling? What are the ingredients of trust and betrayal?

◆ Practice trust and fidelity by doing the trust walk again; play a game where you have to work as a team (charades or Pictionary); write a letter or make a phone call that will reconnect you to someone whom you have neglected.

5.

Go and Do Likewise

I say more: the just man justices;
  Keeps grace: that keeps all his goings graces;
Acts in God's eye what in God's eye he is—
  Christ. For Christ plays in ten thousand places,
Lovely in limbs, and lovely in eyes not his
  To the Father through the features of men's faces.[1]
Gerard Manley Hopkins

The Christian community approaches the good life with the conviction that this life has already been lived by Jesus the Christ. To live the good life today, then, we must creatively embody his way of life in our own situations. We call this being formed as disciples. The disciple is one who learns from a master. Discipleship is not concerned with reproducing point for point the external aspects of the master's life and work. It is concerned, rather, with making the master's wisdom, dispositions, and spirit shape our own character so that we will prefer spontaneously the way of life that harmonizes with the master's.

Recent attention given to the role of mentors in the

process of adult development reflects this insight of discipleship. Mentoring relationships introduce the novice to the values and style of a new social world. Apprenticing to a mentor is an important feature of forming character. So in the moral life, developing Christian moral character is tied to Jesus as the master, the supreme mentor, the exemplary role model. The whole Christian tradition points to him as the source of its vision and virtue.

When we turn to Jesus as the master of the good life, we are following the conviction that the moral life is influenced a great deal by significant persons with whom we identify because their lives fascinate us and capture our imaginations. The Christian moral life takes Jesus as the master. For Christians, he is the most fascinating person informing our imaginations of the way life ought to be lived. In fact, what distinguishes Christian morality from any other is that it relates God becoming human in Jesus to all of human life. The final justification for who we ought to be and what we ought to do is that obedience to the lordship of Jesus demands it. For this reason, Christians look to Jesus as the standard or model for the way the good life ought to be lived. That Jesus ought to be the guiding pattern for our lives is set forth in John 13:34 when Jesus tells his disciples in the context of their final meal together, "Just as I have loved you, you also should love one another." Paul makes a similar appeal when he exhorts the Philippians, "Let the same mind be in you that was in Christ Jesus" (Phil 2:5).

However, there is a major difference between being fascinated with the role models and mentors arising out of our immediate communities of influence and being fascinated with Jesus. We physically interact with our other role models. We see them and talk to them. When it comes to Jesus, we have to deal with the four gospels that tell the story of Jesus, and we have to participate in the life of the church that keeps these stories alive. Christians believe that prayerfully engaging these stories through the Spirit and in the church makes it possible to experience the presence of Jesus again and to see what his spirit looks like in our day.

To be a Christian implies having convictions about the person and work of Jesus. While Christians have often disagreed about how to understand the significance of Jesus, the centrality of Jesus for the Christian life has never been questioned. This chapter will sketch a portrait of discipleship in light of an interpretation of who Jesus is as the model of the good life. I will first present one, admittedly limited, way of responding to Jesus' question to Peter, "Who do you say that I am?" Then, I will draw a portrait of discipleship that responds to the command that Jesus frequently used to close a parable: Go and do likewise.

Who Do You Say That I Am?

Jesus is "in." For so long we have grown accustomed to pledging our allegiance to someone quite unpopular and unappealing, at least if we judge what is popular and appealing by the standards of the marketplace. But that is no longer the case. Jesus is "in." Jesus has exploded on the scene in sight and sound, color and fashion, in ways we could hardly have imagined a few decades ago. To adapt the image from the poet Gerard Manley Hopkins, we can say "Jesus plays in ten thousand places." That is true not only poetically but literally as well. Jesus plays on Broadway, in the movie theater, on home video; Jesus' sayings appear on billboards, bumper stickers, buttons, and T-shirts. Jesus has become a folk hero.

Because many of us grew up at a time when the only proclaimer of Jesus was the church, this explosion of the Jesus phenomenon might leave us a little unsettled and confused, if not embarrassed. But scripture scholars have opened a rich treasury of insight into Jesus, and the pop culture offers fresh ways of thinking about and portraying Jesus. So from every medium and in a variety of images, we are getting startling, colorful, contemporary answers to the question put to Peter, "Who do you say that I am?" (Mt 16:15).

But our age is not unique in this regard. Every age has tried to answer the question put to Peter for its own time. The days of the Roman Empire looked to Jesus and found a formidable other-worldly Christ, like the one we find on icons and in paintings. The Middle Ages saw in Jesus a stern ruler of the Last Judgment, or the crucified Christ of St. Francis. The Puritan Age saw a severe Judge, and the Age of Romanticism turned a rugged carpenter into a pale, rosy-cheeked weakling. Now there is our age. We have known the waxy image of Hollywood in *The Greatest Story Ever Told* as well as the earthy images of *Jesus Christ Superstar* and *The Last Temptation of Christ*, where we meet a Jesus who knew fatigue, depression, uncertainty, and fear. We also have the finger-snapping, toe-tapping image of Jesus as the light-hearted clown in *Godspell*, where we get a sense of a man who took pleasure in the earthy, the rhythmic, and even the giddy.

The impact of the Jesus movement cannot be denied. It is challenging us in ways more effective than most preaching to get clear about Jesus and to take a stand on the question Jesus put to Peter. To help you sort out where you stand on Jesus, I invite you to take this true-or-false test. Here are five statements about Jesus. Where do you stand on each?

—— Jesus liked some people more than others.

—— Jesus was never troubled by life. He was always certain how things were going to work out.

—— Jesus' love had sexual dimensions, and as he

grew up he had to integrate his sexuality into his personality and care for others.

—— The care and love of his parents and friends helped Jesus grow as a person.

—— Jesus' encounter in the desert was a real temptation to give up on his mission.

Look over your answers. What made you take the stand that you did?

By considering these questions and trying to give reasons for the stand you took, you are embarking on the theological effort called christology. This means that you are trying to understand who Jesus was and what Jesus meant and continues to mean for you. The New Testament witness to Jesus sets the tone, the pattern, and the direction for all subsequent interpretations. We find many different ways of interpreting Jesus in the New Testament. He is given titles such as Messiah, Son of Man, Son of David, Christ, Word, Lord, Prophet, Teacher, and others. We also know Jesus through his work as redeemer, sanctifier, and justifier. Together these ways of interpreting who Jesus was and what he did capture some of the richness of the fuller meaning of Jesus. But no title or work alone says it all. When we use all of these interpretations of Jesus, it is as though we were turning a gem around to let it refract different rays of light in order to appreciate its fuller beauty.

For purposes of trying to understand Jesus as the model of the good life, I am going to draw a composite sketch of Jesus (because each gospel refracts different facets of him) in order to discover the Jesus who will show us what the good life looks like.

Jesus is God-with-a-face. As God, he shows the fullest expression of God's self-giving love reaching out to us. As one of us, we see in him the fullest expression of the human response to God's self-giving love. This means that one of the ways we might understand our profession of faith that Jesus is true God and true man is in the action terms of giving and receiving. In this way, we can look to Jesus to know what God is doing in the world, namely, loving us; we can also look to Jesus to know what it means to be human, namely, to give freely in self-emptying love what we have received freely by God's self-giving to us. What makes Jesus the ultimate norm for living the good life is not anything he said or did but who he was and is—the fullest revelation of divine love to us and the fullest human response of self-emptying love in return. The good life for the Christian, then, is not just the imitation of a good man but the imitation of the divine love expressed in Jesus.

In that one paragraph, I have summarized a rather complex christology. I need to explain it a bit. This christology begins its reflection on Earth and so pays great attention to the humanity of Jesus without denying his divinity. This approach to understanding Jesus begins with the synoptic gospels rather than the gospel of John. Its presumption is that only after meeting the man from Nazareth can we come to know his divinity as well. This approach contends that if we are to know anything about the God whom no one has seen, we ought to look first to Jesus in his humanity.

From the perspective of trying to understand Jesus from the ground up, we can assume that when the people of Jesus' time looked at him, they did not say to themselves, "There is God; let's see how God acts." Rather, those who lived with Jesus saw someone much like themselves, someone who shared with them the complexities and contradictions, the satisfactions and disappointments, the joys and sorrows of being human. They saw a man free enough to say what he believed and courageous enough to take the consequences; a man dedicated, yet often frustrated; a man who sometimes went hungry and sometimes dined with the rich; a man who amazed the crowds but couldn't retain the loyalty of one of his own; a man who had a special feeling for those who were hurt or lost, yet who was deserted by his own at the time of his greatest agony; a man whose whole disposition was toward mercy, forgiveness, and nonviolent resolution of conflict, yet who died by capital punishment.

Jesus was different in the unique relationship he had with the Father. The gospel accounts of his baptism in the Jordan convey how Jesus must have experienced himself as someone special in God's eyes: "You are my own dear son. I am pleased with you" (Mt 3:17; Mk 1:11; Lk 3:22). The rest of the gospel demonstrates the practical effect of holding fast to these words of worth received out of the waters of baptism. Central to his identity and security was his "Abba" experience of divine love. The secret of his living a life of self-offering love is his life secured by the divine love of God.

Central to Jesus' teaching is the lesson that his divinity did not in any way denigrate his humanity. In fact, Jesus shows that it is okay to be human. He showed how life can be lived in a world as it is, not in a world of how we would like it to be. He lived a fully human life by being completely alert to the mystery of life all around him, the mystery that was himself, and the mystery that was his Father speaking through all that surrounded him. Jesus showed that we can come to know who God is and what God requires of us by looking hard and deep into our own lives, into the lives of others, and into the land. No wonder Jesus taught the ways of God through images of a rich young man, a poor widow, the blind and the lame, even a doting father with two spoiled children, as well as through mustard seeds, fig trees, stormy skies, and lilies of the field. Someone who tells stories filled with images such as these is someone who has listened to humanity and to the Earth, and is someone who has spent many silent hours in the desert.

Jesus tells us that to be human is to discover yourself and to discover God, more by surprise than by intention. It means that to be human is to live with others and to learn how to love and to be loved, how to be one's own person and still be of service to others. Jesus shows us that really to be human and to live morally is to take responsibility for living. It is not to hitch one's soul to another's star or to do what others say simply because they may have authority over us. Rather, truly moral living is to say what you believe to be true, to do what you believe to be right, and then to live out the consequences.

Like all of us, Jesus grew gradually in his humanity. The gospel of Luke tells us that he "grew in wisdom, age, and grace" (Lk 2:52). He learned to love from the experience of being loved. He learned what it is to have a friend, to receive a gift, to be cheated and laughed at. He knew the feeling of self-worth, trust, and obedience. He learned to pray, to watch, and to listen.

The gospels do not think it strange that Jesus should ask questions or grow in knowledge. To be graced is not to be a know-it-all. In a Charlie Brown comic strip, Charlie asks, "I wonder what it would be like to know that you were perfect?" Lucy responds, "Take it from me, it's a great feeling." I understand Charlie more than I do Lucy, and I think you do too. So would Jesus.

Unlike the Greeks for whom ignorance is simply imperfection, Jesus showed that it is human not to know everything; it is human to discover, to live with surprise and change, to find our dignity in taking our lives into our hands, sometimes to fail but to rise from failure and to try again. When Jesus was in agony in the garden, how could he have hesitated about his death if he already had full assurance from divine knowledge? Was he only faking his feelings when he cried out from the cross? A Jesus who walked through the world knowing exactly what tomorrow would bring is a Jesus who might arouse our admiration but still is a Jesus who is far from us. On the other hand, a Jesus for whom the future is a mystery and a hope, as it is for us, is a Jesus who could effectively teach us how to live, for this is a Jesus who would have gone through life's real trials.

So we do Jesus and ourselves no favors by ignoring his humanity and saying that he knew everything because he was God. Yes, Jesus always was God. But as a human, he had to discover who he was and what God was asking of him just as we do, step by step. How human would he really have been if he did not have to face what we find to be at the core of humanity—the call to search and discover our way through failure and groping and finally coming up with something new? Our great pain and our great joy is in asking "What's it all about?" and gradually discovering the answer. Jesus would not have been truly human and so not much of a model for moral living if he did not have to search and find, either because he knew beforehand what was going to happen in every instance and so could arrange his life with perfect foreknowledge or because he was being dragged through life like a puppet on a string. Jesus was one who tested life and who was tested by life. He searched out life's meaning, listened carefully to what makes life really valuable, and then decided, over and over again, in favor of God's rule of self-emptying love.

Jesus' decisions did not come easily to him even though he shared a unique communion with the Father. He had to spend time in prayer, reflect, struggle with ambiguity and temptation, sweat and agonize over big decisions, take risks and dare. Part of being human is to make decisions on the basis of the best evidence we can gather at the moment and to commit ourselves on the basis of calculated risks and with the character we have formed. Jesus acted on faith in a God he had to try to understand with human intelligence, just as we must. He had to make up his mind what in particular his Father was calling him to be and to do. For example, when people wanted to make him king, he had to decide whether it was a political messiah that he was called to be. He had to decide what to say to restless crowds; he had to decide when it was prudent to take himself out of the public scene for awhile and quilt himself in quiet to pray; and he had to decide when it was time to walk into Jerusalem, dangerous though it might be.

Because Jesus moved through his life by making choices, he knew how difficult it is to make the faithful choice and how attractive it is to hedge on a commitment to the Father and the rule of living by self-giving love. Like any person trying to make faithful choices, he knew the power of temptation to turn away from the consequences of self-emptying love or the consequences of telling the truth. The temptations in the desert were not finished after forty days, never to be repeated. Temptation marked the whole of his life, as it does ours. How could these temptations have been real temptations—the kind we contend with—if there wasn't the slightest possibility that he could fall for them? He was tempted like any of us who struggle to know how costly it is to be faithful. As enticing as the temptations were, he trusted in the word he heard from his Father and refused to give up his freedom or to yield the primacy of love as the rule of life.

Because Jesus made a whole lifetime of faithful choices, he could do nothing but pay the price—powerlessness, loneliness, misunderstanding. For all of his insistence on service, two of his own argued over who was to be the greater. People raised their eyebrows when they saw him talk to a Samaritan woman, and he knew the pain of being rejected because he bore witness to the truth in his own life and to the untruth in the lives of others. Not even his closest friends understood when the crisis came. Aloneness weighed heavily upon him in that hour of prayerful struggle in Gethsemane. He knew then the price of being faithful to the Father. When the showdown came, he became the victim of another's charade of justice and of his own years of freedom and faithfulness.

The freedom and faithfulness that we find in Jesus make a difference for the way we interpret the significance of his life, especially his death. I think it would have made a great deal of difference to the early church, and consequently to the whole Christian tradition, had Jesus died of natural causes or in his sleep. The crucifixion makes clear that his life of faithfulness was a free choice; his execution was not an unexpected occurrence or something that just happened to him. It was the consequence of who he was—a sign of contradiction to those who resented him and wanted him killed. The freedom of wanting to do what we do is the freedom that enables us to take our life into our own hands and to stand with our decisions. Such freedom is not the prerogative of only great people in history, it is also for us.

When the power of evil was at its mightiest, Jesus loved and he hoped. He plunged into death with a question on his lips, "My God, why have you forsaken me?" but also with hope in his heart, "Into your hands I commend my spirit." He died as he lived—trusting that life was not a bad joke and that his questions about life would not echo into an empty future. He died as he lived, believing in himself because he trusted that God believed in him. Because he was receptive to the gift of life both around him and in him as coming from the Father, he broke the grip of suffering and death for himself and for us, and his Father raised him up.

Jesus died with no proof that resurrection would come. He died hoping the God in whom he trusted would bring a radiant future. The hope of Jesus is not grounded in a guarantee but in a risk. Jesus took a risk on having his life filled with the mystery of God. This hope allowed him to live as though his life were not in vain. Jesus took a risk on life filled with divine love, and he took a risk on a God of surprises. We celebrate his surprise as Easter. Without hope, we would be terrified by anything new or uncertain. We would put off deciding, or we would only be able to decide half-heartedly for fear of the results or for fear that life was rigged against us. The resurrection of Jesus signifies the future for anyone who is free and hopes in the God of surprises.

Ultimately, the story of Jesus is the story of God and how God is present to us. Jesus tells us where to look for the presence of God. What he tells us is to look into the depths of our humanity, into the world, and into the communion of people living for one another a life of self-emptying love. The imitation of Jesus is not simply to accept obediently any of his commandments, nor is it to repeat the externals of his life as though we were invited to an exercise in nostalgia. Authentic imitation is to take seriously what he took seriously—free and faithful loyalty to the Father, which showed itself in a life of self-offering love committed to those most in need of justice and liberation. The question that ought to guide authentic discipleship today, then, is not "What would Jesus do?" but "How can I be as faithful to God in my life as Jesus was in his?"

Go and Do Likewise

A collage of gospel stories of the life of Jesus gives us a picture of what the spirit of Jesus is like and who we might become in imitation of his freedom and his faithfulness. Because Jesus knew himself to be special in God's sight, he did not have to strive for greatness or latch onto false loves in order to secure his identity, his position, or his power. We become disciples by following the way of renunciation (Mk 8:34). We have to let go of the attachments and illusions that enslave us, such as prideful desire for recognition to secure our worth, a crippling fear of rejection for not being worthy of love, a selfish attachment to our present position in life, a slavish conformity to go along with what everyone else seems to be doing or thinking, or an attachment to money, material possessions, power, or prestige. Unless we learn to give up the presumption that we can ensure the significance of our lives by creating these surrogate loves, we are not ready for discipleship.

To be a disciple demands the freedom to let go of whatever so occupies our hearts that we have no room for divine love. The call to be a disciple is a call to leave all and to follow Jesus. It includes giving up family and its affection (Mt 10:37), property (Mk 10:21), ambition (Mk 10:43), and even life itself (Mk 10:45). In sum, the disciple is to let go of all forms of self-made securities in order to be secured in divine love!

Jesus lived his life out of a heart that treasured God. As the gospels have it, when our hearts treasure God, all other treasures will be treasured rightly (Mt 6:21; Lk 12:34). The Lukan Jesus aptly summarizes the implications of a heart so filled with divine love: "Of what the heart is full, the mouth will speak" (Lk 6:45). Words and deeds are but the heart in paraphrase. Jesus lived with his heart set on doing what he understood the Father to be asking of him. In being so faithful, he lived free of false loves so that he could embrace the whole world in love as he understood the Father to be doing. As disciples, we are to go and do likewise.

Perhaps the most challenging of gospel stories calling to the radical renunciation of discipleship is the story of the rich young man (Mt 19:16–30; Mk 10:17–31; Lk 18:18–30).

The young man asks Jesus what he must do to share in everlasting life. Jesus tells him to keep the commandments. The young man says he has kept them all his life. But being a law-abiding citizen does not make for discipleship. Something more is required. Jesus looks at the young man with love and invites him to give up all those things on which he has come to rely for status, security, worth, and well-being and to follow Jesus. At that, the young man's face falls. He goes away sad for he has relied on many things.

What is it about the rich young man that makes it impossible for him to share fully in divine love? We get a hint from a Peanuts cartoon that finds Linus sharing his hopes with Charlie Brown. Linus says, "So I've decided to be a very rich and famous person who doesn't really care about money, and who is very humble but who still makes a lot of money and is very famous, but is very humble and rich and famous." Charlie looks at him in amazement and says, "Good luck." Charlie has it exactly right: "Good luck" if you try to live with a heart set on more than one thing. The challenge of discipleship is to make God the focus of our loyalty and hope so that everything else will fall into proper perspective. What makes being a disciple difficult for the rich young man is that he wants to hang onto his home-made securities as the source of his worth and lovableness. Jesus invites him to let go so that his heart can be filled with divine love. Jesus invites us to do likewise.

Because Jesus knew himself to be loved by God, he did not have to strive for greatness, demand the center of attention, devise strategies of self-defense, or force others to think the way he did. Jesus as seen by Matthew's community, for example, says that true disciples are to avoid all known techniques that would secure positions of superiority in their religious and social community. They were not to use religious dress (to broaden their phylacteries or to lengthen their tassels) in order to attract attention. Nor were they to take the reserved seats in religious assemblies that symbolized superior roles in the community. They were not to use titles, such as rabbi, father, or master, that require others to recognize one's superior status (Mt 23:5–10); in short, they were not to dominate in the name of service. The way of Jesus is the way of service—leading without dominating, inviting people to change without shaming, intimidating or forcing them to think the way he did. We are to do likewise.

Jesus' singular devotion was to do the Father's work of setting people free and inviting all into communion with God and with one another. His miracles, for example, are great works of liberation. His parables are often judgments on the use of power to exclude. Jesus was free in himself and from himself so that he could be inclusive of a great variety of people despite the features that made many of them outcasts to their own people. If we are to be disciples in the spirit of Jesus, then we must do likewise—be free enough in ourselves to nurture moral sensitivities that have a special concern for those who are hurt or lost, that make room for the stranger and the outcast, that are disposed to act toward others with mercy and forgiveness, that seek the nonviolent resolution of conflict, that are inclusive of all, and that challenge any striving for superiority over another.

There is perhaps no more memorable scene in all the gospels that illustrates the character of discipleship than the foot-washing scene at the Last Supper. This story from John 13:6–10 is used as the gospel reading on Holy Thursday in conjunction with the Pauline text of the institution of the Eucharist (1 Cor 11:23–26). When taken in that context, coupled with our understanding that it takes the place of the institution narrative of the Eucharist in the gospel of John, the action of Jesus in washing feet highlights even more the character and style of discipleship.

In this scene, when Peter sees Jesus, the master, acting like a servant, he knows something is out of place. This is not the picture Peter has in his imagination of the structure of relationships in the community. So Peter resists being washed. He realizes that if he were to comply with the washing, he would be accepting a radical change in the way he ought to relate to others. The action of Jesus is challenging in a radical way the structure that makes some superior while others remain inferior. Such a conversion is more than Peter is willing to undergo. When Jesus deliberately reverses social positions by becoming the servant, he witnesses to a new order of relationships in the community and to a style of being a disciple wherein the desire to dominate has no place. When Peter finally allows himself to be washed, he accepts the call for him as a disciple to do likewise.

To many of us, the call to be free and faithful in the way Jesus was is a call to a radical way of life. It seems so far out of reach. The seemingly unattainable life of a disciple only reminds us that we are all works in progress. We are always letting go and learning to love with hospitable love. While each of us will live as a disciple in a way that corresponds to our openness to the Holy Spirit, the call to discipleship invites us to go beyond where we are now, to open ourselves to divine love, and to live as friends. It is to the characteristics of the life of this community of friends that we turn next.

Spiritual Exercises

◆ In a quiet place, repeat the title of this chapter, "Go and do likewise," as a mantra or breath prayer. Rest with this for a moment.

♦ How do you answer the question Jesus put to Peter, "Who do you say that I am?" Share your Christology with a small group.

♦ Select the one gospel passage that best expresses for you who Jesus is. If you do this exercise in a small group where each can share a text and explain what made you choose it, you will begin to get a complex portrait of the Jesus who continues to be the model of the good life today.

♦ Now do the same exercise with a passage expressing what discipleship looks like for you. Again, if you can do this in a small group, you will come away with a richer portrait of discipleship.

♦ Page through a book of Christian art. Stop at the picture that expresses your image of Jesus. Do the same for your image of discipleship. Share with your group what strikes you about this depiction of Jesus and of discipleship.

♦ We are asked as disciples to be as faithful to God in our life as Jesus was in his. What is this call to be faithful demanding of you at this time in your life, in your family, in your workplace?

6.

I Call You Friends

After Jesus comes the church. We cannot become disciples all on our own. If it were not for the church, the community of disciples, we would have no access to Jesus at all. We learn discipleship by being initiated into it by others. To be like Jesus requires that we become part of a community pledged to be faithful to him. Unless we establish strong bonds of solidarity with others who share in friendship with Christ, we will not be able remain committed to discipleship. We need flesh and blood instances from which to learn what friendship with God involves and how discipleship might be lived every day.

To live the good life, we need a community of friends to sustain us by their example, wisdom, encouragement, support, and challenge. The church is to be such a community. This means that church membership is far more than the passive acceptance of doctrines or the submission to a set of precepts. Belonging to the church, rather, is an adventure of following Jesus in new and ever-changing situations. The church is to give the world a hint of what life looks like when we take God's love to heart and Jesus' vision of discipleship into the home, the workplace, and the marketplace.

This chapter will provide a profile of the character and virtue of the community called by the word of Jesus to witness to God's love. That community becomes friends with one another and with God by accepting the reign of God and its corresponding virtue—hope—and by living according to the radical demands that the reign of God makes on the moral life—that is, by being a beatitude people whose love for one another is characterized by forgiveness and hospitality.

The Reign of God

As Jesus called his first disciples in the midst of their everyday lives to change their hearts and to commit themselves to the vision and values of the reign of God (Mk 1:14–15; Mt 11:29), so he again calls us. Jesus' proclamation of God's reign does not refer to a geographical place of acres of real estate with rustic villas, serene mountain lakes, and colorful meadows; rather, it is his dream of the way the world ought to be. The "reign of God" is a dynamic, relational reality whereby each person lives with God as his or her center of loyalty and experiences a strong sense of solidarity with others. In this sense, when we pray in the Lord's Prayer, "Your kingdom come...," we are not praying that a geographical kingdom literally come to us, but we are praying for a life where God is at the center and justice and peace prevail among us.

When we put God at the center, all other authorities in our lives will be seen in their proper relation to God. The justice that we hope will prevail in our relationships with one another and with the Earth is a condition characterized by a strong sense of belonging to others, of cooperating with one another's gifts, and of empowering relationships of mutuality, equality, and inclusiveness among persons and between us and the Earth. The peace that we hope will prevail is not simply the absence of conflict, but it is living together without the fear of being destroyed. Such a community of peace can only come about not by violently seeking revenge to even the score but by making sure that forgiveness and reconciliation are always within reach. In a peaceful community we will live trusting in the goodness of one another and creating hospitable space where the gifts of others may flourish to nourish the life of all.

The parables of Jesus express in a compelling way what life under the reign of God is like. Taken as a whole they disclose the profile of the moral character of one who lives under the reign of God's love. This character is marked by reverence, conversion, and responsibility.

Reverence is the capacity to pay attention, to turn our taken-for-granted world on its head, and to be open to surprises. In the life of a disciple, there is no substitute for seeing, recognizing, and hearing those who are part of our lives. Hatred is not the opposite of reverence. Indifference is. In Arthur Miller's play *Death of a Salesman*, Willy Loman's wife seems to understand the crucial role of reverence and recognition, for she pleads the case of her desperate husband this way: "He's a human being, and a terrible thing is happening to him. So attention must be paid. He's not to be allowed to fall into his grave like an old dog. Attention, attention must be finally paid to such a person." She knows that anyone who goes unnoticed not only feels invisible but actually falls out of the picture. If attention calls us to life, its absence drives us to death. The Samaritan also displays reverence in seeing the man in the ditch from the inside of his feelings and experience. He knows what it is like to be a victim. He has been there himself. Because of reverence, the Samaritan sees through social divisions to a relationship of mutuality. Reverence keeps us open to what is really going on.

Conversion reorients our way of seeing, thinking, feeling, judging, and acting. It is a foundational experience in the life of a disciple and has a central place in Jesus' proclamation of the reign of God (Mk 1:15). Conversion suggests change; but after we have spent so much time trying to get our lives together, who wants to face the call to change? No wonder conversion meets with so much resistance. It disturbs our being at home in the world we have created on our own terms. It involves the process of being thrown off balance and then being restored to balance on a new basis. We see this aspect of conversion vividly portrayed in the life of St. Paul. Before he abandoned his life as a persecutor of Christians and became the apostle to the Gentiles, he "fell down" (Acts 9:4; 22:7; 26:14). When he got up, he was on the way to a whole new life. As a continuous process, conversion means that we are likely to be thrown off balance more than once.

The conversion called for in the life of a disciple is a transformation from the inside out. The change of heart blossoms into a change of vision, attitude, and conduct. To be converted means to see things we have never seen before, to think new thoughts, to hold to new convictions, and to do new deeds all because we have awakened to a deeper love orienting our lives. But conversion that does not lead to a commitment to social action is not authentic conversion. We are social through and through. The test of conversion is the quality of loving service that we render to our neighbor. The Samaritan expresses conversion in being moved by what he sees. The sight of the man beaten and lying abandoned in the ditch shocks his imagination with a fresh image of what being neighbor means. His conversion is heart-deep and socially oriented, for out of the depths of his feeling comes healing action.

Responsibility is directed toward acting under the reign of God where love knows no limits. When we act responsibly, we are cooperating with divine love. To the extent that we cooperate with God's grace, our actions help people to live under the ultimate authority of God in justice and peace. Cooperating with divine love means that we continually call into question and seek to reform oppressive and dominating structures of human existence so that everyone may live as sisters and brothers in a community of inclusion, equality, and mutuality. The Samaritan acted responsibly when he saw through the social divisions between Jews and Samaritans and lifted his neighbor out of the ditch.

Hope

Hope is the central virtue of those living under the reign of God. Hope is rooted in the confidence that life is more reliable than unreliable because all possibilities for life and its future are under the care and goodness of God. As simple as it sounds, hope expects a happy ending, even when there is no particular good thing left to hope for. What is our ground for such hope? Simply, the good news of Christian faith that God's love for us is undefeatable. This is most evident in Jesus' being raised from the dead. Our ultimate warrant for hope is the resurrection of Jesus, the best of all possible futures. Founded on the love of God and the resurrection of Jesus, hope frees us to live with confidence in the power of good to break into each particular place.

Hope is a heroic virtue today. Cynics see it as a curse that breeds passivism, keeping alive the will to live when life is painful. But hope is not to be confused with an easy optimism or dismissed as wishful thinking. Hope is not a lazy kind of escapism. It trusts that the future is open, that new possibilities for life exist, that we are not fated by blind necessity, that we can change, and that tomorrow can be different from today. With confidence in the possibility that those things that are now destructive of human well-being and fellowship can be restrained and changed, hope challenges us to live together and work together for peace and justice. Knowing that "this too will pass" is the wisdom of hope. It enables us to remain open to the possibilities for new achievements. Hope allows us to avoid despair when we come face to face with our personal and social sinfulness because hope knows that a part is not the whole.

In hope we do not have to proceed with the determination to make sure that everything turns out right. Hope assures us that all will be well no matter how things turn out. Hope enables us to find meaning in whatever happens because hope rests on the faith conviction that all is sustained by the graciousness of God. For this reason, too, hope keeps the disappointing pieces of life from swelling out of size and blocking the channels of change. In hope we can lean on the future trustingly with the expectation that something good will happen. Hope honestly admits that the good that comes is gift; for if we had all the power to bring about the good, it would make little sense to hope for it.

Because it always points to the love of God as the basis for the fulfillment of new possibilities of human well-being, hope is the source of our energy to respond creatively to new possibilities for recreating society. Knowing that we are accepted by God and that God will never abandon us, we have the courage to take the steps we need to take in order to build a community of justice, love, and peace.

Being a Beatitude People

The charter document for the life of the community of disciples is Jesus' Sermon on the Mount (Mt 5—7). This sermon begins with the familiar beatitudes and then continues with a series of radical demands that express the absolute claim that God has on anyone who lives under God's reign. The sermon is addressed to those who have already heard the proclamation of the reign of God and want to make this offer of divine love the total basis of their lives. We are those people today.

Let's try to hear the beatitudes freshly, then, for they present a portrait of the sort of people who are to make up this community of disciples. In these beatitudes we hear Jesus express what it means to be human in the way he sees it and lives it. Here we learn something more about what it will mean to live as one especially chosen to follow Jesus and to contribute toward living in a community of friends where justice and peace reign.

I will present each beatitude with a brief commentary that highlights the moral and spiritual challenge it holds. Perhaps you can read this section reflectively as an examination of conscience.

1. Fortunate are those who know they are spiritually poor; the kingdom of heaven belongs to them.

To become the sort of person Jesus was means that we have to be able to accept that all that we have and are comes as a gift from the Father. To recognize the fact that the foundation of our being is not in ourselves but in God is to know our ultimate dependence. This is real poverty—to know that we are ultimately dependent on God's graciousness. We are not masters of the universe. We will always live dependent on God and interdependent with one another. Poverty is knowing that we can't go it alone, that we have needs, that we don't have it all together yet, and that we never will. But some of us have to be at the end of our rope before we know how poor we are.

2. Fortunate are the gentle; they shall receive what God has promised.

The gentle and the meek are those who can make room for someone else. They are not so arrogant or self-centered that they see only what they want to see or hear only what they want to hear. The meek and the gentle can be open to what is without having to manipulate or control, and they are free enough to let go of hanging on to self-centered securities so that they can be embraced by the ones who are dear to them. They even have enough space in their lives to accept another's faults without bitterness and to admit to their own without regret.

3. Fortunate are those who mourn; God will comfort them.

Those who mourn are fortunate because they can accept their own emptiness before God. They are content with who they are—no more, no less. In their own emptiness they can grieve over the suffering of others, feel the pain of another, walk in another's shoes. Like the mother of Jesus and the beloved disciple at the foot of the cross, those who mourn stand by the excluded and the suffering, offering them, if nothing else, the support of their witness.

4. Fortunate are those whose greatest desire is to do what God requires; God will satisfy them fully.

We are fortunate if we have high ideals, strong values, noble goals, and the motivation to build up what is best in ourselves and to draw out the best in others. Yet, the temptation to conform, to be like everyone else, to be satisfied with being average is never far away. But those who build up an appetite for God feel the urge deep within themselves to develop their gifts and to share them for the sake of the well-being of others. As Mother Teresa expressed it, they feel drawn to do "something beautiful for God." They are free enough to forget self for the moment and to let others approach in their loneliness and distress and even in their hope and enthusiasm.

5. Fortunate are those who show mercy to others; God will show mercy to them.

It is a mercy that God loves us, and it is mercy that distinguishes the disciple's life. Merciful love is compassion without conditions. Mercy is being sensitive and responsive without being defensive. Mercy is not indifferent, does not hold grudges, does not enjoy criticizing others. Those who are merciful are full of care for others knowing that God is full of care for them.

6. Fortunate are the pure of heart; they will see God.

How happy we would be if we could take off our masks, be free of false images, and simply be the persons we are. To be pure of heart is to be single-hearted. It is not to have hidden agendas or secret desires to advance ourselves when dealing with another. The pure of heart can congratulate and support another without seeking to advance themselves. They are not envious of another's successes, nor do they ridicule those who live out of their heart's desires. Because the pure of heart have set things right on the inside, they can see the presence of God on the outside.

7. Fortunate are those who work for peace; God will call them his own.

"Peace be with you," says Jesus (Jn 20:19). St. Paul tells us that by his death on the cross, Jesus united two—Gentile and Jew—into one with himself, thus making peace. Those who work for peace help others to live in harmony rather than with division; they show people how to cooperate rather than compete. They do not brood over hurts; they let go. They do not live satisfied with walls that rise up between them and others; they build bridges.

8. Fortunate are those who suffer persecution because they do what God requires; the Kingdom of heaven belongs to them.

The cross of Jesus is a sign of victory, not defeat. We celebrate the cross as a sign of life. The persecution suffered from another's displeasure or jealousy should not stop us from witnessing to what is right and good. When we live under the sign of the cross, we can find courage to suffer for our convictions, and we can accept hostility and anger without trying to hurt in return those who do not see things our way.

Love One Another

Following the beatitudes in Matthew's gospel are further instructions that reflect the values of Jesus and dramatize the quality and direction which ought to characterize the Christian moral life under the reign of God. How often we hear it said, "That wasn't a very Christian thing to do," or we say in praise, "She has such a Christian attitude." What are we noticing in that person's character or actions that makes "Christian" an apt qualifier? Certainly it would have something to do with being loving. But the fuller teaching of Jesus on the moral life asks of his disciples something more than living by the Golden Rule. We are to go beyond merely doing to others what we would want them to do to us. Jesus' teaching on love includes the command to love our enemies and to pray for our persecutors. In fact, how we treat our enemies is the key test of whether we love our neighbor. The lifestyle of the disciple is to be marked by nonviolence and nonretaliation. Not even the restraint of taking "only" an eye for an eye is acceptable here. Love is not to seek vengeance at all! It is to give generously without seeking restitution. These dimensions of love are probably the most distinctive features of Christian morality.

What makes it possible to live this way? Martin Luther King, Jr. suggests how in one of his sermons about loving enemies:

Let us be practical and ask the question, How do we love our enemies?

First, we must develop and maintain the capacity to forgive. He who is devoid of the power to forgive is devoid of the power to love. It is impossible even to begin the act of loving one's enemies without the prior acceptance of the necessity, over and over again, of forgiving those who inflict evil and injury upon us. It is also necessary to realize that the forgiving act must always be initiated by the person who has been wronged, the victim of some great hurt, the recipient of some tortuous injustice, the absorber of some terrible act of oppression. The wrongdoer may request forgiveness...like the prodigal child...but only the injured neighbor, or the loving parent back home, can really pour out the warm waters of forgiveness.[1]

Another American who had to struggle with this teaching of Jesus about loving your enemies is Terry Anderson, one of the Americans held hostage in Iran for six and a half years. If there is anyone who has been challenged to love his enemies, he certainly was. He says this:

> We can't separate the thing we do from what we are; hate the sin and love the sinner is not a concept I'll ever really understand. I'll never love him—I'm not Christ. But I'll try to achieve forgiveness, because I know that in the end, as always, Christ was right.[2]

"But I'll try to achieve forgiveness." That is the spirit with which we try to respond to the teaching of Jesus as well. I suspect that when it comes to fulfilling the command, "Love your enemies," we are all still on the way, still trying, still in need of conversion. What motivates us to strive to forgive is the love or mercy of God that we are to imitate: "Be merciful as I am merciful." The Christian life, remember, is not just the imitation of a good man, Jesus; it is the imitation of the divine love expressed in Jesus.

Forgiveness is central to the teaching of Jesus. His very mission was about the forgiveness of sins. In a world where people seem to be trying constantly to get even, forgiving does not come easily—at least so it seems in the experience of most people. Two obstacles get in the way of forgiving: one is fear; the other is our lust for power.

The unforgiving person is generally full of fear. Often this is the fear of being hurt again. The fearful person builds walls instead of bridges in relationships. Bridges make one vulnerable; walls protect by keeping the other separate and apart. Forgiveness breaks down walls and brings us closer. But coming closer is precisely what we fear. Coming closer makes us too vulnerable. After being hurt once, we are too frightened ever to make ourselves vulnerable again.

The other obstacle is our lust for power, the desire we have to hold something over someone else and to make their hurt against us the filter through which we relate to them. When we refuse to forgive, we assume some kind of position of superiority that says to the offender, "You owe me." And so the unforgiving person is always trying to even the score, to get revenge. That is why refusing to forgive is one of the great destructive behaviors of our times. But revenge distorts the right relationships that we ought to strive to achieve. Revenge denies any shared responsibility for the wrongdoing. It cultivates victimhood as an identity and so traps us in anger and resentment. Revenge believes that the only way to address evil is by imitating it, and that triggers successive waves of violence.

We can learn a great lesson about forgiveness and revenge from Herman Melville's Ahab in *Moby Dick*. On one whaling voyage, Ahab had his leg bitten off by Moby Dick, the great white whale. The wound, especially the senselessness of it, so maddened Ahab that he spent his whole life in mad pursuit of the offending animal. But at the end of the book, when Ahab plunges his harpoon into the whale, he only succeeds in tangling himself in the rope and is pulled into the sea where he drowns. The lesson: forgive, or the past will rule your life and the anger and resentment that you harbor as a victim will lead to your own ultimate destruction.

Forgiveness is an essential part of achieving justice in the community. Revenge frustrates justice. This came to mind as I watched more and more television reports and interviews of family members and others involved in the trials of Timothy McVeigh and Terry Nichols concerning the

Oklahoma City bombing, and of Theodore Kaczynski, the unabomber. I mourn for the rage, anguish, and depression of those who lost loved ones in these bombings. I also acknowledge that these deeds were heinous crimes and that those responsible ought to be punished. They have lost their right to move about freely and to participate fully in society. But this does not mean that they have no right to life whatsoever.

Punishing evil deeds such as these is a way of showing that there are some forms of behavior that are unacceptable for people living in society. If public morality were to become so riddled with relativism that we could not even condemn monstrous evils, then we would surely lose crucial reference points for any dialogue on how we ought to live together. So it is important that we are able to say that some behaviors are clearly wrong and out of hand in our society.

While we have to protect ourselves from people who do monstrous evil, I cannot understand how, in a country with as many Christian churchgoers as ours, so many people believe that revenge will bring them justice. Any position founded in any way on revenge is at serious odds with the gospel. I don't understand how we can continue to listen to the stories of Jesus and still act as if killing killers will somehow make everything turn out right. There is nothing in our Christian tradition that says violence is redemptive. Evil is not conquered by evil; death is not overcome by another death. Executing criminals only further brutalizes society and makes it easier to take human life in other circumstances. We are missing the message of Jesus when we continue to put more faith in violence than in mercy.

Because of obstacles like fear and power, with their insidious lust for revenge, we have to force ourselves to forgive. It doesn't come naturally. The first step toward forgiveness must take place by a conversion of heart. If it is true that how we feel is influenced by how we think, then when two people separate, their reunion will depend on the thoughts each has had about the other while they were apart. To achieve forgiveness we must first begin to think differently about our offender before we can speak and act differently toward him or her.

Next comes letting go. The Greek word we translate as "forgive" (*aphiemi*) means "to let go." But this step is hard. We want to hang on to our resentments. We are like the monkeys in the following story who are captured in a very ingenious way. Their captors take a gourd or pumpkin and hollow out the inside, cutting a hole just big enough for a monkey's hand to squeeze through. Then they throw peanuts inside the pumpkin, tie it to a tree, and leave. When all is quiet, the monkeys investigate, smell the bait, reach in to get the peanuts, make a fist, and then try to get free without letting go of the food. But the opening is too small for the fist to get out, and the only way they can hang on to the peanuts is by making a fist. So they are stuck. The next day, they scream with rage and fear as their captors pick them up and ship them off to the zoo forever. If they would only have let go, they would be free. The lesson: to forgive we have to let go of something. If our hands are full of the hostility that the past has engendered, of our own superiority, of our need to be in the right, or of our need to control, then we can't let go; we can't forgive.

Forgiveness that lets go requires more than simply saying, "Ah, just forget it." Contrary to popular opinion, forgiving has little to do with forgetting. The popular advice that says "forgive and forget" can easily encourage us to see forgiveness as a form of denial. Such advice ignores the past and tries to carry on as if what has happened is of no importance. But forgiveness doesn't require that we forget what happened. In fact, forgiveness begins with remembering the wrongs that have been done, calling them by their proper names, and honestly acknowledging the results. We don't pretend that nothing happened or deny that it was wrong; instead, through forgiveness we resolve not to let what happened in the past keep us frozen from moving into the future. We know that we cannot remake the past; it is over. We will always carry the past and its effects with us into the future. The question is, "How will we carry it?" Will we drag it as a ball and chain that makes moving into the future difficult? Will we carry it as a weapon ready to use against someone else? Will we hold it as a shield to protect us from ever being hurt again? Forgiveness that lets go of the past turns the past wrong into an occasion to learn, to grow, and to create a future. Forgiveness makes us free to move beyond hurt and anger and toward reconciliation.

Letting go of our investment in the past in order to move into the future is symbolically expressed in the story of Jesus forgiving the paralytic. Jesus forgives the paralyzed man and then commands him to pick up his mat and go home (Mk 2:1–12). The forgiveness acknowledges the past—you did wrong—but it looks forward—let's go on from here. Forgiveness can move on from the past hurt because it acknowledges that there is more to the offender than the offense. What makes this hard is that it involves loving the something more in people in spite of their offense. Forgiving depends on a higher level of perception that allows letting go of the offense in order to embrace the offender. It will not let the hurtful event of the past control the rest of one's life. The past must be reworked, not deleted from memory. If we forget, we risk exposure to the same offense. The remembering, however, is not a reminiscing or brooding over the past. Remembering is a recollecting, a seeing anew, a reintegrating of the past into one's self-understanding with an acceptance that sets us free.

Finally, in time, forgiveness awakens the true potential for good in the other. At this stage, one has let go of trying to be superior to the other and of holding power over the other. Awakening the good in the other is a move toward reconciliation—we walk together again because we stand on equal footing and enter into a mutual relationship once again. Forgiving enables the other to move from self-centeredness and fear to the self-forgetfulness and freedom that builds bonds of friendship and community.

I Call You Friends

Jesus' command of love is tough. People throughout the ages have tried to make it work. Some have died for it; almost all have known the discouragement of trying to make it work. It asks for more than a random act of kindness, and it certainly asks for something more than being nice or occasionally thoughtful. It demands loving those who are most difficult to love because they have hurt us. It demands that we forgive "seventy times seven times." Of all the attempts to bring some clarity to the kind of love that is commanded, I have found those that explore the notion of hospitality to be most helpful.

Stop here for a moment to think about what hospitality means to you. When you have extended hospitality, what did you do? When you have received hospitality, what did you receive? What did it feel like? I wonder how closely your ideas compare with mine.

My ideas draw on two of my favorite biblical stories about hospitality. The stories tell of the marvelous things that can happen when we create a welcoming space for another. They tell us that guests carry precious gifts with them and are eager to reveal these gifts to anyone who would create a safe and sacred space for them.

My favorite Old Testament story of hospitality is that of Abraham's receiving three strangers at Mamre (Gn

18:1–15). As the story goes, these strangers reveal themselves as the Lord, announcing that Sarah, even in her old age, will give birth to a son. By welcoming the strangers, Abraham discovers how the Lord's promise to him will be fulfilled. The author of Hebrews gives us the lesson of that gesture for all times: "Remember to welcome strangers in your homes. There were some who did that and welcomed angels without knowing it" (Heb 13:2).

In the New Testament, my favorite story of hospitality is the Emmaus story (Lk 24:13–35). Two travelers to Emmaus invited the stranger who had joined them on the road to stay with them for the night. As the story goes, Jesus made himself known to them as their Lord and Savior in the breaking of the bread. In both stories, hospitality to the stranger becomes the opportunity for the strangers to reveal their most precious gifts and for the hosts to discover something special about themselves. Through hospitality, separations and distinctions evaporate in the rites of communion.

Hospitality, however, should not be limited to the gesture of receiving the stranger. It needs to become a fundamental attitude and action that we express toward one another. It has two important dimensions. One has to do with power, the other with presence.

Hospitality does not seek power over others. Cruelty does. Cruelty deliberately causes harm, especially crushing a person's self-respect. Cruelty manipulates relationships whereby the stronger becomes the victimizer of the weaker. Hospitality, however, risks vulnerability to take a chance on the other and on the possibility that the other may change us. It creates a safe space to welcome another in with trust and affirmation and so restores a sense of worth and communion. This space is not merely a place to be. Above all, it is fostering an environment, providing relationships that allow another to feel at home. In an hospitable environment, one is free from the preconceptions and judgments that distort one's perception of what is going on or of who one really is. As a result of hospitality, community is possible.

Hospitality is also about presence, and the key to being present is "paying attention." Isn't it curious that we speak of *paying* attention? What is the price of attentiveness? Time and self-forgetfulness. This high price of attentiveness is what makes hospitality such a rare virtue.

Hospitable attention is not like making a cocktail party contact, where we fill the time until someone really important comes along. Rather, the recognition of attention is like the reverence that characterizes the disciple: it displays genuine interest in the other for the other's sake and not just as a useful contact whom we can use to make other useful contacts. Paying attention with sensitivity and responsiveness is not as easy as it seems. It is a real asceticism. We are usually overeager to push our own agenda without first paying attention to what the other needs. We are often like the boy scout who saw an elderly woman with arms full of groceries at the street corner. He quickly took the groceries from her, firmly grabbed her arm, and guided her across the street. As the boy gave the woman back her groceries, she politely said, "Thank you, young man, but I was waiting for the bus. Could we go back across the street now?" Perhaps this kind of spirit of helping is the reason the Buddha said, "Don't just do something; stand there!"

When we pay attention, we make a deliberate, conscious effort to resist imposing our ideas about how things should be and, instead, let what is before us make its impact on us. This kind of paying attention requires that we divest ourselves of our self-preoccupations. Prayer is the discipline of attentiveness and the school of hospitality. In prayer we pay attention to the world outside us as well as to the world inside us. Indirectly, then, we are paying attention to God and creating space for God's love to transform us.

To be hospitable to God, to other people, and to the world, we have to get out of ourselves and become interested in the other. We have to create that space where others can feel safe, experience new bonds of communion, and rejoice because someone has finally made room for them and accepts them. My favorite metaphor of the virtue of hospitality comes from my former mentor, Fr. Jim Dunning, who embodied this virtue well, but unfortunately died much too soon for more people to experience this virtue in him:

> Each of us is like a rock with walls and barriers that keep others out and keep us secure. But year after year God keeps carving away at our rock. One day we discover that God's hand has created some empty space in our rock. He has been chipping away at us and now we discover a cave hewn out of stone. We find we have some space to welcome people in, people who are also weary, tired, and in need of some space in which to gather so that they will not feel alone. They come in and say to us, "Oh, I see you have been doing some rock dwelling, too. The carving hand of the Lord has also been chipping away at your grand design and your plans and ambitions. I see you have some empty space. Perhaps I might come in. You know what I have been through. Perhaps you can hear me. Perhaps you won't force your plans on me, manipulate me, or try to control me. Perhaps you will offer a place where I can be me."

This metaphor is expressed in other words in the gospel of John, especially Chapters 13 and 15. There we find the Johannine version of what this metaphor of hospitality looks like. In the foot-washing scene in John 13, Jesus demonstrates the distinctive characteristic of this love as the mutual self-giving that breaks down relationships marked by the superiority of a few and the inferiority of all the rest. Jesus establishes a relationship built on mutuality and equality.

In the great discourse of Chapter 15, Jesus no longer calls his disciples servants but friends because he has abolished their inferiority to him and shares with them everything he has received from the Father (Jn 15:12–17). The paradigm for human relationships that Jesus proposes for his community of disciples is friendship. Jesus summed up the witness his life had given when he said to his disciples, "I no longer call you servants...but I have called you friends because everything I have heard from my Father I have shared with you" (Jn 15:15). Jesus' final command to his disciples is to love one another as he has loved them, that is, with the love of friendship (Jn 15:12).

This Johannine friendship is what it means to create hospitable space in order to receive another and to experience new bonds of communion. It creates a community of mutual interdependence among its members so that people are not locked in a ceaseless competitive struggle to dominate everyone else. It is, instead, a community where people come to life through gentleness, mercy, and sacrifice. It is where everyone is willing to put their gifts at the service of everyone else. Friendship creates a community where there is mutual challenge and correction to nurture the life-giving potential in each but not to diminish, destroy, or stifle the creative contribution anyone can give. It is a community that seeks to enhance the dignity of each and not manipulate, maneuver, or exploit anyone. It is a community that governs itself without recourse to power that coerces, controls, dominates, divides, or does violence in any way. It is a community where people can live in the peace and harmony necessary for a mingling of souls and a unity of spirit. As friends, such a community of disciples becomes united with the mission of Jesus to use its power so that all may have life in abundance. No one ever remains a stranger or an enemy for those who live by such hospitable love of friendship. It is in the friendship of such a community that the good life takes shape.

Spiritual Exercises

◆ In a quiet place, repeat the title of this chapter, "I call you friends," as a mantra or breath prayer. Rest with this for a moment.

◆ What makes hope such a heroic virtue today? What/who makes you hopeful? Check the newspapers for signs of hope.

◆ Read the beatitudes again. You might try to use a translation that is new for you so that you can hear them freshly. Which of the beatitudes is especially challenging for you? What do you understand it to be asking of you? Pick one to practice this week. If you can share this exercise in a group, and each person happens to select a different beatitude, you will go away with a richer picture of the demands of discipleship for today.

◆ Forgiveness is the concrete expression of loving our enemies. Examine the relationships around you. You might want to return to your concentric circles from earlier chapters. Is someone trying to forgive or seek forgiveness but is meeting with resistance? What dynamics are going on in this relationship that makes forgiving difficult? How can you be a peacemaker in any of these relationships?

◆ Share with the group what you try to do when you offer hospitality. Practice hospitality: pay attention; make space in your heart and in your mind for someone else's point of view; make space for God by creating a quiet place in your life; invite guests to your house and celebrate them.

7.

The Good Life

"Tell them what you're going to tell them. Tell them. Tell them what you've told them." So went the advice I was given in my first course on public speaking. It applies to writing as well. It is time to bring these reflections on the good life to a close. Because the telling has spread over several chapters, it may be helpful if I try to sum up and round out the central ideas that the previous chapters have proposed for integrating the moral and spiritual life in our quest for the good life—a virtuous life that requires companionship with others to make it possible.

To summarize the previous chapters about the moral and spiritual life, it is wise to follow the sage advice which says, "First things first." St. John reminds us what this is in the case of the good life: "This is what love is: it is not that we have loved God, but that God loved us" (1 Jn 4:10); and again, "You did not choose me, I chose you" (Jn 15:16). In matters of morality and spirituality, God makes the first move. As the spiritual masters have taught, we would not be searching for God if God had not already found us. Our whole life is lived in response to the love we first receive as a gift of God's graciousness. Although every love can change us, only God's love can change us into God's friends. The good life is a life of friendship with God and all that God loves—ourselves, other people, and all of creation. Of course, when speaking about our friendship with God throughout this book, I am speaking analogously. We will never have a friendship with God exactly like the friendships we have with others. The friendship we have with God is friendship of a sort. Its possibility arises not in us but in the offer of God's love that makes the moral and spiritual life possible in the first place. Another, and perhaps a more familiar way of talking about becoming a friend of God is to talk about becoming holy or becoming a saint.

Because the good life means living as a friend of God, the moral and spiritual life must come together. The point of convergence is in a person's character and virtue. Throughout this book, I have assumed that we act the way we do largely because external conditions challenge us to reveal the habits we have formed, the beliefs we hold, the ideals we aspire to, the image we have of ourselves, and our perceptions of what is going on. We rely on our strength of character and virtuous habits to appreciate what is at stake, to distinguish the degrees of importance among values, and to discern appropriate responses to the situations we face. What we regard as a problem and how we ultimately respond to what is going on will depend a great deal on the sort of persons we have become. So when moments of special choice come along, we tend to choose automatically, as it were. In a sense, we have already made the really important decisions. They lie in our identity. For these reasons, I have been more interested in the character and virtue that we bring to whatever problems we face than in how to solve problems.

The focus on character and virtue shows that when we

live from day to day, we are not just doing something that accomplishes a goal, like picking up the kids at day care, paying our bills, or driving patiently through the rush hour traffic, but we are also becoming someone—more loving or selfish, more gracious or stingy, more patient or anxious, more aggressive or defensive, and so forth. One of the key insights of virtue ethics is that how we do something affects the kind of person we become (our character) and, in turn, the kind of person we are affects how we act. If we do things well, we become better; if we do them poorly, we become worse. It is like athletic training: if we swim well, we become better swimmers; if we swim poorly, we become worse.

Perhaps the greatest predictor of how we will behave when moments of special choice come along is to be found in how we behave every day because daily behavior shapes character. In everyday living, the way we do things affects the person we become. If we drive like a maniac, the chances are we will become one. If we treat our co-workers in a condescending manner, the chances are we will become arrogant and patronizing and so treat others in a condescending manner as well. In turn, the person we become influences what we see going on and readies us to respond in a certain way. If we habitually tell the truth, we not only become a truthful person but we also develop a special insight enabling us to recognize what truthfulness and deceit mean in concrete circumstances. We don't expect the cowardly suddenly to do a brave deed or the Silas Marners of this world to break into fits of generosity. Shakespeare's *Macbeth* shows that you can't go about creating a life of villainy and not be affected by it. The scene of Lady Macbeth trying to wash out the imagined spots of blood on her hands is a very powerful expression of how our actions become so much a part of ourselves that we can't make a clean separation of who we are from what we do. If we want to make the virtuous choice in a hard situation, we will need to develop the habit of doing the right thing in smaller affairs. In the biblical idiom, the good tree brings forth good fruit; the evil tree brings forth evil fruit.

The kind of person we bring to a situation makes a great deal of difference for how we interpret what is going on and for how we behave toward it. For example, why is it that two people facing the same bleak prognosis of a debilitating condition will respond differently? They do so because they have different moral characters that influence the way they interpret what is going on and how to behave toward it. One person might see it as unmitigated, meaningless suffering; the other may see it as part of the fragility of human life and as a time for letting go into the hands of God. Their different interpretations reflect their different characters. The difference is explained by how their morality and spirituality work together.

The good life, then, is not about living in a world separate from our ordinary life. The good life is a life that we can live within the very activities and responsibilities that fill our days. The quest for the good life is about living virtuously in companionship with others.

From the point of view of the Christian believer, to live the good life means to grow in our fullness as disciples of Jesus and to respond to the presence of God in a way that leads to full communion with God. There is no other way to come in touch with the life of discipleship than through relationships with those who share in it. We cannot become good without those who also share in our quest for goodness. The character and virtues of the good life require a stable, enduring relationship with those who share with us what we consider important about life: thus the importance of the church as a community of friends. The church can give the world a glimpse of the kind of life that is possible when we take God's love for us to heart. In our life together, we should be able to demonstrate that violence is not inevitable, that living in harmony with the earth is possible, that selfishness can be overcome by generosity, and that care, compassion, and kindness are the ways to call people to life.

In short, the good life is not something we can achieve on our own. It takes friends. Becoming virtuous is a cooperative adventure. We cannot become good persons apart from relationships with people who also want to be good, who share our aspirations, and who love us enough to help us achieve them. Whatever goodness we achieve is not so much the result of our own efforts as it is the handiwork of friends who draw the best out of us.

Building an approach to the good life around friendship, however, is not easy in a culture that trivializes and subverts friendship. The good life requires friendships that grow out of a place in ourselves where we know that we are loved. But what so often passes for friendship in our culture grows out of a need for affection and affirmation. What we call friendships are often superficial acquaintances or co-dependent relationships of manipulation. Moreover, friendship is easily jeopardized by consumerism that leads us to believe that we need things more than people. But, as the bumper sticker reminds us, "The best things in life are not things." In a consumer society, our identity is too easily measured by our riches and not by the richness of our love. We can too easily make friends just another commodity to pick up, use, and dispose of as we see fit.

Then there is the ethos of individualism. It sees the self not as social and relational but as private, disconnected, autonomous, and self-sufficient. It suggests that the more independent we are, the better off we are. It says that people are more likely to take life from us than to give it. It sees others more as threat than as gift. In its radical form, individualism undermines the fundamental requirement of friendship: the awareness that each friend wants what is best for the other and will work to secure it.

To live the good life, then, we need others in our lives who share our sense of the good and are committed to seeking it with us. To grow in the good life, we need people who share our dreams, ideals, values, cares, and concerns. We need people who agree with us about what matters most in life, especially about what is worthy of loving. Robert Coles reminds us in *The Moral Intelligence of Children* of how not just children but all people acquire moral character. He says that children acquire a "moral intelligence" not only by memorizing rules but also by watching how adults behave: "The child is a witness; the child is an ever-attentive witness of grown-up morality—or lack thereof."[1] Then Coles goes on to make an observation about his own experience of acquiring character as a doctor:

> I remember myself as a young doctor, and as a witness to that elder doctor; I remember *his* "moral intelligence"—his respect for other people as well as himself, the deep awareness he acknowledged of our human connectedness. I was a witness to how he approached his patients, hurt and ailing children, but also their parents, and us interns, residents, nurses, and as well, the orderlies and nurse's aides and volunteers and janitors, all of whom make a hospital run smoothly and all of whom he took pains to acknowledge with consideration, respect....

> He didn't give lectures and sermons as to how we interns and residents ought to behave with one another, with the hospital staff, with the children we were treating. Nor were we handed articles to read,...In fact, he *said* very little to us; he lived out his moral principles, and soon enough, we were witnesses to his behavior, to his ways of being with others, which we were challenged to absorb, as all young

people are inclined to do, when they have learned to admire and trust someone older: try to follow suit.[2]

What Coles seems to be telling us is that to become good, we need to be surrounded by goodness, to witness it, and then to imitate it, or as the young brother said to his older brother, "When I grow up, I want to be just like you. Please be better."

While the number of friends that a person can have is limited, what we learn through them about ourselves and about relating to others will have effects far beyond the boundaries of special friendships. As Robert Coles's experience of his physician-mentor illustrates, being in the company of good friends teaches us how to be with others, to care for them, and to be genuinely interested in other people. In other words, friendship with a few teaches us how to be friendly toward many.

Being a friend of God and of all that God loves comprises a way of life constituted by a whole set of virtues, some of which have been explored in this book.

We are made in the image of God. As icons of God, we are sacred and social. As sacred, we have **dignity** beyond our achievements. Our dignity is both a gift and a responsibility. As social beings, we live the good life by giving freely what we have received freely so as to create a community wherein everyone can flourish.

Humility is the virtue that expresses the realistic acceptance of our gifts and our commitment to do what we can. Even though we can't do everything, we try to create a community of sisters and brothers characterized by equality, mutuality, and reciprocal giving and receiving for the sake of the well-being of all.

Gratitude is the virtue of remembering that all comes as a gift to be shared and not as a possession to be hoarded. Gratitude looks over life, not to find what is missing, but to notice that who we are is largely the result of the handiwork of the care and support of friends.

Self-esteem is the virtue grounded in accepting the original blessing of being loved by God. It makes the good life possible because it enables us to enjoy being who we are and doing what we can to build bonds of friendship.

Justice is the virtue that sets relationships right. It makes it possible for people to live in harmony with one another and with the Earth. Justice reaches out to include those who can easily be forgotten—the lost, the least, the last.

Solidarity is the virtue by which we are determined to live and work with and for one another and in harmony with the Earth. It enables us to see others as partners sharing in our common humanity; to judge how our plans and projects have an impact on those most in need; and to act with and for those who work to make society a community of justice, love, and peace.

Fidelity and **trust** are the virtues that enable us to live together as friends and to build bonds of communion that last. These virtues enable us to take a risk on the goodness of another and to receive one another more as gift than as threat.

Hope is the virtue that enables us to live in a discordant world without losing meaning, purpose, or direction. Hope lives with confidence in the possibility that those things that are now destructive of human fellowship can be restrained and changed and that, no matter how things turn out, we will be able to make sense of it all because we are sustained by a fundamental graciousness that cares for us.

Forgiveness makes the call to love our enemies concrete. It is the virtue that makes it possible for us to live with one another without letting revenge and violence dominate our life together.

Hospitality is the love that gives expression to all the other virtues. It is the practice of paying attention to what is going on around us and then creating a welcoming space where we can experience new bonds of communion and live with all who are willing to put their gifts at the service of everyone else.

This in brief is a sketch of the sort of persons we need to become to live the good life. It takes friends to become this sort of person. Without friends we remain moral midgets and spiritually bankrupt. But what kind of friends do we need to sustain us? I want to close this vision of the good life with some characteristics of the kinds of friends we need so that we can become friends of one another and of God.[3]

We need friends who will challenge us to stay focused on what is true about being made in the image of God and called to live together in justice, peace, and love. We need people in our lives who will help us to see ourselves sincerely and challenge us to be true to who we are, to do the best that we can, and not to pretend to be who we are not. In his first volume of poetry, Robert Frost included a short poem called "Revelation." He ends by saying:

> But so with all, from babes that play
> At hide-and-seek to God afar,
> So all who hide too well away
> Must speak and tell us where they are.[4]

We are among those "who hide too well away" from ourselves. Hence the need for friends who tell us where we are. Such are the friends who will help us to look at our lives and ask, "Who am I listening to now?" and "Are you doing the best that you can?"

Along with those who challenge us, we also need those who will cheer us on. These are the people who are so crazy about us that their love frees us to be our best selves, to take risks on our own giftedness and that of others. These are the people who are ready to encourage us when our unrealistic expectations of ourselves and others threaten to pull us down. These are also the ones who, after an experience of hurt or disappointment, hold us in their hearts and some-times in their arms, to let us know that we are loved more than we are hurt. These are the ones who let us see our-selves reflected in their face and give us the confidence to see our errors and limitations in more accepting ways. Instead of seeing them as proofs that we are bad, these friends help us to see what we still need to accept for the truth it reveals about us but not as being the whole of who we are.

We also need people who will help us to laugh. A sense of humor keeps perspective, heals our attitudes, and re-stores us to a healthy balance. Through humor, we can understand, appreciate, and even embrace those puzzling, mismatched events and occurrences that permeate our life. There is enough sadness, misery, and gloom in life. But do we have enough humor to offset the heaviness? A good friend disposes us to laugh, first at ourselves; and when we are the first to laugh at ourselves, it seems like our idea! Anyone can laugh at another's stupidity, but it takes a spe-cial gift (a friend) to recognize our own folly. Being able to laugh, especially at ourselves, brings us down to earth where we can be at home again with our own vulnerability. When we are with someone who laughs at himself or her-self, we know how quickly we feel at ease with ourselves as well. Their perspective is contagious; their laughter infec-tious. We begin to laugh, too. It is freeing, relaxing, and even healing. Friends who help us to stay in touch with our humanity, maintain our enthusiasm, and keep our perspec-tive are a rare gift indeed. But these are the kinds of people we need in our lives if we are going to live in a way that enables everyone to live a richer life becoming friends of one another and of God.

Spiritual Exercises

- In a quiet place, repeat slowly, in a mantra fashion, the word *good*. Notice what emerges for you; what images, experiences, people, feelings come to you. Rest there a moment. Now do the same with the word *life*.

- Reflect on your experience of friendship. Make a list of those who nourish you with their love and support. Who in your list challenges you to be your best self? Who celebrates you, even when you are not at your best? Who gets you to laugh at yourself?

- Is there an image or biblical text that captures the heart of friendship for you? Share this image or text with a friend. Does your image or text ring true to them about their experience of you?

Notes

1. What You Have Received as Gift, Give as Gift

1. As found in William J. Bausch, *Storytelling: Imagination and Faith* (Mystic: Twenty-Third Publications, 1984), pp. 135–136.

2. Viktor Frankl, *Man's Search for Meaning*, trans. Ilse Lasch, rev. ed. (New York: Simon and Schuster, 1962), p. 65.

2. I Have Called You By Name; You Are Precious to Me

1. Edward J. Farrell, *The Father is Very Fond of Me* (Denville: Dimension Books, Inc., 1975), p. 5.

2. Fyodor Dostoyevsky, *The Brothers Karamazov*, trans. Constance Garnett (New York: Signet Classics, 1957), pp. 56–57.

3. I Will Be Your God, and You Will Be My People

1. As found in Robert Coles, *The Moral Intelligence of Children* (New York: Random House, 1997), pp. 10–11.

2. This threefold movement is more fully developed in Fred

Kammer, *Doing Faithjustice: An Introduction to Catholic Social Thought* (New York: Paulist Press, 1991), pp. 147–159. This book is a valuable resource to explore further the themes in this chapter.

3. Gregory Baum, *Compassion and Solidarity* (New York: Paulist Press, 1990), p. 58.

4. *I Desire Faithfulness, Not Sacrifice*

1. This comparison of the two gardens is based on John Shea, *The Challenge of Jesus* (Garden City: Doubleday & Co., Inc., 1977), pp. 9–113.

5. *Go and Do Likewise*

1. Gerard Manley Hopkins, "As kingfishers catch fire," *The Poems of Gerard Manley Hopkins,* edited by W. H. Gardner and N. H. Mackenzie, fourth edition (New York: Oxford University Press, 1967), p. 90.

6. *I Call You Friends*

1. As found in Kathleen Hughes and Joseph A. Favazza, eds., *A Reconciliation Sourcebook* (Chicago: Liturgy Training Publications, 1997), p. 122.

2. Ibid., p. 95.

7. *The Good Life*

1. Robert Coles, *The Moral Intelligence of Children* (New York: Random House, 1997), p. 5.

2. Ibid., pp. 5–6.

3. I am building here on the insight of Robert J. Wicks, *Touching*

the Holy (Notre Dame: Ave Maria Press, 1992), pp. 96–108. This book is a complement of what I have tried to do here.

4. *A Pocket Book of Robert Frost's Poems* (New York: Washington Square Press, Inc., 1964), p. 155.